MAGICK IRL

SARA CALVARESE

Copyright © 2022 Sara Calvarese-Allen, The 8th House LLC
All Rights Reserved

FOREWORD
SO WTF IS THIS BOOK, ANYWAY?
The short answer...I suppose it's my love letter to the study of the astrological and tarot archetypes, but it's also more than that.

If you're reading this book, then you probably already know that I am (was?) a scientist. You probably also know that I think of science and spirituality as not being mutually exclusive. In fact, I would argue that the two are more similar than different. At their core, they share many of the same goals. They both aim to make sense of the world, they both want to improve our quality of life, they both wish to provide us with a sense of choice and personal agency, and they both use the information we know to extrapolate information we don't.

Scientists studying chemical reactions or the migratory patterns of birds are not really all that different from astrologers studying planetary movements. The larger cycles that make those chemical reactions and migratory patterns so predictable are also the same cycles that put a little pressure on all of us around age 29 when transiting Saturn returns to its exact placement in our natal charts (we'll talk more about Saturn Returns later in the book). The point is, the cycles already exist, doing what they do. Science and spirituality are just our way of marking time, documenting the patterns, and using our collective historical understanding to make sense of the complex world around us.

All time is human assigned. We came up with the concept of the Gregorian Calendar. We decided that a year is 365 days based upon the Earth's orbit. But, truthfully, how we measure time is both meaningful and completely arbitrary. It's significant in the sense that this is how we live our lives. It's how we denote special days. It's how we know when we have an appointment. It's how we communicate our age to someone. However, our measurement of time is also arbitrary in that a year could have been assigned to be 600 days instead of 365, and we could have decided that a day was 15 hours instead of 24. It wouldn't change the natural cycles. It would just change the way we track and describe them.

Astrology and tarot are precisely like this, both entirely meaningful and arbitrary at the same time. They are meaningful because they represent specific universal cycles and archetypes, but they are altogether human assigned to explain the patterns around us and mark time.

This means that the planets and the tarot don't "make us" do anything. Yes, you read that correctly. We have all the personal agency and free will in the universe. But, both are powerful tools to help us make sense of the world around us, just like science.

Astrological and tarot archetypes represent the entirety of the human experience as we know it, independent of all the many things that divide us. None of us is an exception to them. I mention this because we live in a time where more and more people are discovering and fostering a connection with various spiritual or "witchy" practices. However, we also live in the age of social media, where a follower count and a curated and aesthetic feed are used or often mistaken as "credentials" or "expertise." The truth is, there are no experts where access to these archetypes is concerned. They are universal. The truth is also that real life is messy, and we exist in late stage capitalism, at least in the US. Buying the most expensive spiritual tools and having the most perfectly-curated altar may get you noticed on social media, but it's not a requirement to study these archetypes and integrate them into your daily life. The actual "good stuff" is embedded in all the mundane shit we experience every day. Don't believe me?

If you've ever felt deeply nostalgic while listening to an old mixed tape you found when you were cleaning out your basement or garage, you've experienced the 6 of Cups. If you've ever accidentally hit "reply all" to a work email, you may have been acting under classic Knight of Wands haste. Or maybe you're someone who gets really into Halloween and loves to go all out with scary movie marathons, trips to haunted houses, and over-the-top spooky decor. If this is you during October, you have experienced the witchy and otherworldly magick of the sun transiting through Scorpio, an archetype associated with death and underworld, among other things.

So, what is this book? It's a not-so-woo exploration of the many-layered tarot and astrological archetypes and how they connect. It's also an invitation to explore many relatable, real-life ways we experience and engage with the larger natural cycles in the universe.

BEFORE WE GET STARTED, THERE ARE A FEW THINGS TO MENTION...

THE FUNDAMENTALS

TAROT AND ASTROLOGICAL LINKAGES ARE NOT AN EXACT SCIENCE, ESPECIALLY WHERE COURT CARDS ARE CONCERNED. THIS IS A BIT OF A DEBATED TOPIC IN THE WITCHY COMMUNITY. I'M INCLUDING THE RATIONALE FOR THE ARCHETYPE LINKAGES WE'LL BE USING BELOW. IF YOU'RE FROM ANOTHER SCHOOL OF THOUGHT, DON'T @ ME. JUST KIDDING! IT'S TOTALLY COOL IF YOU LOOK AT THE MODALITY OR ELEMENTAL MATCH-UPS DIFFERENTLY. I JUST WANT TO MAKE SURE I PROVIDE THE BASIS FOR HOW THE BOOK IS STRUCTURED AND HOW THE EXERCISES ARE ORGANIZED.

Now, let's talk layers. We can look at linkages between tarot and astrology in a number of different ways. Understanding the many archetype overlaps and connections helps us solidify our grasp on the concepts. It's kind of like knowing how to derive a formula in math or physics (because you comprehend the foundational tenants on which it's built), as opposed to simply memorizing it. The more connections we build, the greater our ability to apply the concepts in practical ways.

PLANETARY RULERSHIP

We'll be using Modern Rulership for this book. I'll be sure to mention traditional rulers if you're interested in exploring those as well. I'll also be lumping in the planetary rulers and their associated tarot archetypes within their corresponding zodiac sign section. If none of this makes sense to you, don't worry. It's just astro jargon that describes which planets "like" or "support" each sign and house. You can check out page 7 for some quick reference materials.

ELEMENTAL MINOR ARCANA CONNECTIONS

The model we'll be using to describe elemental connections to the Minor Arcana is as follows:
- Wands are Fire Energy
- Pentacles are Earth Energy
- Cups are Water Energy
- Swords are Air Energy

We'll also add the Aces of all Major Arcana to the Cardinal Sign Sections since Aces are initiatory, just like Cardinal Sign Energy.

A WORD ON GENDER, HIERARCHY, AND THE COURT...

I don't like to gender the court cards. But, I do understand that Page, Knight, Queen, and King are the "universal common language" for the court. So, for the purposes of this book, we'll refer to them in this way. But, please be aware that court cards are not hierarchical nor specific to any gender, and we'll be talking about them in a non-gendered way. I'm a firm believer that one of the main reasons people struggle with the court in tarot is because that the cards are heavily gendered. Thinking about the court (or any tarot archetype) in this way is incredibly limiting. It's rooted in bio and gender essentialism. It also ignores the fact that gender is a social construct, and we all experience all of the tarot independent of where on the gender spectrum we fall.

COURT CARD CONNECTIONS: ELEMENTAL AND MODALITY ASSOCIATIONS

The model we'll be using to describe elemental connections to the court cards is as follows. I'm aware that not everyone universally agrees on these. However, here is no right or wrong answer here, and this will be the model used for our purposes.
- Pages are Earth Energy
- Knights are Air Energy
- Queens are Water Energy
- Kings are Fire Energy

The model we'll be using to describe modality connections to the court cards is as follows:
- Kings are Cardinal
- Queens are Fixed
- Knights are Mutable
- Pages will be considered Cardinal*

*Pages aren't always included when we match up court cards with their respective modalities. But that feels incomplete to me. So, I'm going to be lumping them in with the Cardinal/King connections since Pages are initiatory, just like Cardinal Sign Energy. I look at this like this: Pages are the "fresh baby" aspect of Cardinal energy, and Kings are the "mature and sustaining" aspect of Cardinal energy.

COURT CARD CONNECTIONS: STAGES OF LIFE + MATURITY

> In our model, we'll be using the stages of life to describe connections to the court cards as follows.
> - Pages are Childlike/Past Energy
> - Knights are Teen/Adolescent Energy
> - Queens are Adult Energy
> - Kings are Elder/Future Energy

Quantum theory tells us, despite our limited perception of time and space, that neither are linear (thanks, Theory of Relativity!) Also, Block Universe Theory suggests that all time could be contained in a 4D model. Meaning every moment of our lives (past, present, and future) is already out there in spacetime. So, what does this mean with regards to tarot, and more specifically, the court? I like to think of the court cards as a bit of inter-dimensional conversation with the past, present, and future versions of ourselves and other folks we knew, know, or will eventually come to know. It's a mindfuck, I know. Theoretical physics is wild, y'all.

The maturity associations with the court, as I have them listed in the bubble above, aren't new. Most readers think of the court in this way. The terminology "page, knight, queen, and king" isn't inherently a problem either. The issue is the societal biases that we bring to the terminology, as they relate to gender, maturity, and hierarchy. For the model we'll use throughout the book, we will attempt to release and reframe some of those biases.

When we consider that all time is happening simultaneously, that would mean that somewhere out there, a past version of you is out there doing past version of you things, and somewhere out there, a future version of you already knows how you will die. So, what if the court cards were like little inter-dimensional messages from past, present, and future versions of ourselves - a way to give ourselves insight and share something we've forgotten or aren't seeing or can't know yet?

So, instead of interpreting the King of Wands as "a person possessing leadership and drive," what if we looked at it as the future version of ourselves showing up to say, "Hi, I'm the fiery innovator pioneer version of you from the future, and I'm here to tell you that even though your idea sounds unlikely and impossible...do it anyway. You are an authority unto yourself." That's way more powerful, isn't it?

NATURAL/FLAT CHART ASSOCIATIONS

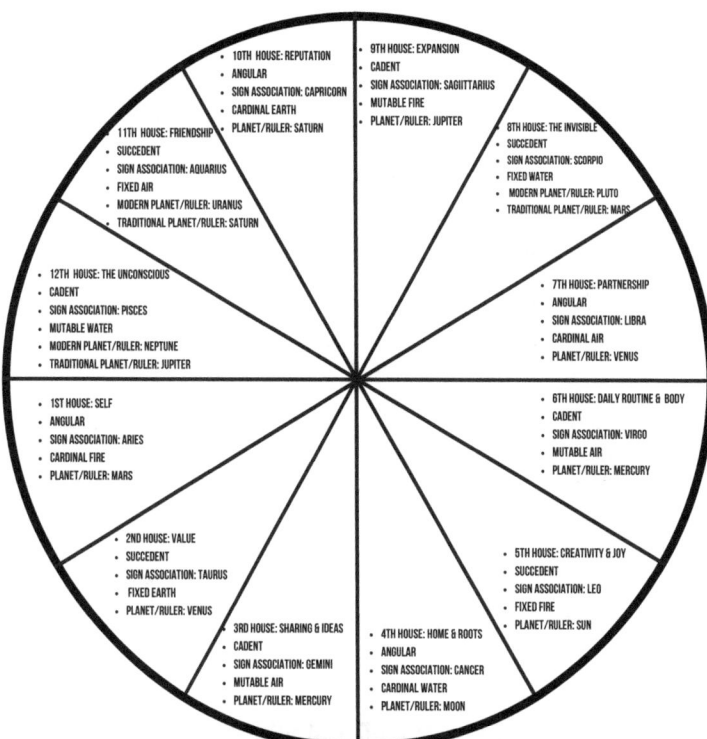

PROFECTION YEARS

Profection years represent the annual advancement we experience based on our age. With every passing year (on our birthday) we focus on development in a new house in the chart. See the brief guide to the right.

HOUSE	AGE	FOCUS
1	0, 12, 24, 36, 48, 60, 72, 84, 96	SELF, BODY + BEING
2	1, 13, 25, 37, 49, 61, 73, 85, 97	FINANCES + VALUE
3	2, 14, 26, 38, 50, 62, 74, 86, 98	EXPRESSION
4	3, 15, 27, 39, 51, 63, 75, 87, 99	HOME + CONNECTION TO ROOTS
5	4, 16, 28, 40, 52, 64, 76, 88, 100	FINDING & FOSTERING JOY + CREATIVITY
6	5, 17, 29, 41, 53, 65, 77, 89, 101	HARD WORK + STRUCTURE
7	6, 18, 30, 42, 54, 66, 78, 90, 102	MERGING + COMMITMENTS
8	7, 19, 31, 43, 55, 67, 79, 91, 103	RELEASE, REBIRTH, + TRANSFORMATION
9	8, 20, 32, 44, 56, 68, 80, 92, 104	EXPLORATION + EXPANSION
10	9, 21, 33, 45, 57, 69, 81, 93, 105	REPUTATION, CAREER, + PUBLIC IMAGE
11	10, 22, 34, 46, 58, 70, 82, 94, 106	SUPPORT FOR HOPES & DREAMS + SOCIAL LIFE
12	11, 23, 35, 47, 59, 71, 83, 95, 107	THE SHADOW, INTUITION, + THE UNCONSCIOUS

ARIES

- DATES: MARCH 21 - APRIL 19
- ELEMENT: FIRE
- MODALITY: CARDINAL
- RULING PLANET: MARS
- HOUSE: FIRST
- PHRASE: I AM
- GLYPH: THE RAM
- TAROT CARDS: ACE OF WANDS, 2 OF WANDS, 3 OF WANDS, 4 OF WANDS, PAGE OF WANDS, KING OF WANDS, THE EMPEROR, AND THE TOWER

ARIES SEASON PLAYLIST

USE THE CAMERA APP ON YOUR PHONE TO ACCESS THIS PLAYLIST.

ARIES - A BRIEF INTRODUCTION

If Aries had a tagline, it would be a blend of "I'm baby" and "Come at me, bro." In all seriousness, Aries energy is dual in nature. There's a beautiful simplicity and directness to Aries, but also an instinctive complexity, and that's something Aries isn't usually credited with. Aries starts the beginning of the astrological "New Year." Our Gregorian calendar may begin on January 1st, but astrological calendars are assigned a bit differently.

Aries is the stuff of fresh beginnings and raw Martian energy. You know the feeling. It's the "I'm sick of waiting, let's just do something already!" feeling. It's anticipation. It's that fire in our guts when we're angry, or turned on, or excited, or maybe even jealous. It's that feeling when our heart races. It's quick to anger but also quick to forgiveness. Being of cardinal modality, Aries is responsible for kicking off its season, and being the first season in the astrological new year, Aries is the pioneer. It's accountable for blazing its own trail since no other signs come before it - the very definition of a true innovator.

Aries' special skill is clearing stagnant energy. This is why we tend to think of Aries as being blunt or impulsive. It may mean saying the thing that needs to be said that no one seems to be saying. It may mean leaving a job or a relationship that is no longer serving us. It may mean picking up and relocating our life on a whim. Yes, this can read as impulsivity, but Aries knows better. It's in touch with what drives us. Its ruler, Mars, prioritizes movement. It's about picking up on instincts and actioning them, no questions asked.

When the Sun is in Aries, we're all illuminated with Aries energy. We're seeing the last bits of winter melting away and the potential of spring emerging. We're sensing that It's time to stop hibernating, and it's time to get back out into the world. It's a time of fresh beginnings, new projects, and zest for life.

In the pages that follow, we'll delve into real-life ways we can invoke the magickal Cardinal Fire of Aries in our everyday lives during Aries season. So, ask yourself: What needs clearing? Where am I craving a fresh start? What am I excited about? How can I take up space in the world?

Turn the page, and in true Aries fashion, let's get it going already...

ARIES (IRL)

Aries comes after Pisces in the wheel of the year. We'll talk about our fishy friend in-depth later, but the critical thing to note about Pisces is that it's one of the most empathetic signs in the zodiac. We can leave Pisces Season so tuned into the needs of others that sometimes we can forget our own. It's not a coincidence that Aries Season comes along immediately after to remind us of the importance of focusing on the self. Pisces zeroes in on the interconnectedness of everything, and Aries is here to call us back into our bodies to get us back in touch with our personal desires. As we move through the sections of this book, you'll find that the order of the zodiac archetypes is deliberate. Each sign evolves and builds on the sign before.

Ok, so it's no surprise that Aries is not exactly known for its patience or follow-through. To be fair, follow-through isn't a Cardinal sign's job. Cardinal signs are designed to be initiatory. Aries loves the excitement of a new idea or a fresh start, and the stereotype of Aries going full force at a new project and then losing interest shortly after has some truth to it. Of course, all stereotypes are based on SOME truth, right? But, this is Magick (IRL), so what I'm interested in here is: How can we use this knowledge about Aries to our advantage in real life? Aries Season is a fabulous time to start projects. Specifically, it's a great time for short projects. Have you been putting off painting that room in your house? Or maybe you've been saying for months how you want to purge your garage. Use the Martian energy to your advantage! This energy is ideally suited for short-lived activities that require a lot of our energy - the more physical, the better. Mars, Aries' ruler or steward, loves anything that gets the body moving!

This is also a season to be direct and bold. Aries is ambitious. It's that feeling of "wanting to make our mark" upon the world. It's about confidently taking up our space. So, Aries Season is a great time to inquire about that promotion or ask out that person you've had a crush on. It's not a time to skirt around issues. Be direct. Ask for what you want. Know your worth. Take up your space. I know. For many of us, this goes against our societal conditioning to people please and "be nice," but Mars is the warrior archetype. Being a warrior requires courage, and Aries Season is when we muster it up and go after what we want. In the pages that follow, you'll find some exercises to hopefully help you clarify what exactly you want and empower you to gather up the courage to channel your boldness during Aries Season.

MEET MARS

We know Mars as the God of War in mythology. This red planet is the steward to the primal fire in all of us, and it's responsible for our ambition, assertion, aggression, action, desires, and passion. Mars takes 687 days to complete its orbit. This means that it spends around two months in each sign of the zodiac and that we experience a Mars Return roughly every two years. A planetary return describes when the transiting planet in question passes directly over the exact zodiac sign and degree where it is found in our natal chart. So, for instance, let's say someone's natal Mars is at two degrees Gemini. Then, roughly every two years, when Mars moves over two degrees Gemini, this person would experience a Mars Return.

So, why are Mars Returns important? They denote where and how we'll focus and expend energy over the subsequent two years. These returns mark the cycles that work to bring us closer and closer to our goals and ambitions and help us determine where to focus our energy.

Suppose you're someone who has an Aries sun or ascendant (or a Scorpio sun or ascendant, under the traditional rulership model). You may find that your Mars Returns are especially significant to the trajectory of your life since Mars is a ruler of these signs. We all experience Mars Returns, and they're meaningful for all of us, but folks with placements in their chart that closely tie them to Martian Energy may find that they experience these shifts in a more pronounced way. Hey, we all have our thing.

Mars helps us clarify our vision for ourselves. It's interested in and prioritizes progress and movement. It helps us carve out and "defend" the space we wish to occupy in the world. Mars is both constructive and destructive. It drives us to build and also to destroy. Let's be honest. Both creation and demolition require strength and courage. That's the very essence of Mars. It's brave, bold, and brash.

This planet is responsible for our guts and our backbone. This is Martian energy. It's how we "get fired up." However, it's important to note that raw drive can be beautiful, but simultaneously dangerous. When we're under Mars' influence, we tend to act first and think later. So, one of the biggest things to watch out for when we're under the influence of Mars energy is that we use it in a healthy and not harmful way.

IT'S JUST A PHASE...
ARIES SEASON MOONS (IRL)

> During Aries Season, we typically experience an Aries New Moon and a Libra Full Moon.

ARIES NEW MOON

New moons are typically a time for fresh starts. When we are in an Aries new moon, it's a great time to get in touch with what pisses us off. Our anger teaches us a lot about our value system. It tells us what's important to us. So, dig deep, and let your rage inspire your next move or project in the world. It's also a great time to think about what excites us. Remember, Aries energy is adolescent and highly excitable. Spend this portion of the moon cycle getting in touch with what ignites real passion in you and how you might like to actively begin pursuit of a related goal. Aries new moons are incredibly potent for planning bold, fresh starts since Aries is the first sign of the astrological new year and one of the most daring pioneers in the zodiac. Use all that fiery energy to your advantage!

LIBRA FULL MOON

Full moons are typically a time for wrapping things up and preparing for release. Libra full moons remind us of the duality between "I" (Aries) and "We" (Libra). Libra deals with themes of balance as well as harmony in our relationships. During Libra full moons, we are often tasked with learning to see things in shades of gray rather than black and white. Libra loves balance. It loves to examine the nuance in all things. The Libra full moon is an excellent time for relationship work, specifically analyzing our differences with others and trying to see the world through their eyes. Venus rules Libra (along with Taurus), and Venus loves art and creativity. So, whatever your preferred medium, Libra full moons can be a fabulous time for release via creativity - artwork, writing, and music are all great choices. If you're someone who is into rest-based self-care, the Libra full moon is also a fabulous time to indulge in that (however it looks for you). Anything to help us feel more balanced is a solid choice for the Libra full moon.

WELCOME HOME
THE 1ST HOUSE (IRL) - THE HOUSE OF SELF

Aries is associated with the 1st House. It's often referred to as the "House of Self," and the main areas of focus for Aries Season and the 1st House are: our sense of self, our bodies, and the identification and pursuit of our personal desires.

The sign that sits on the cusp of the 1st House in our natal chart is what we refer to as our ascendant or "rising sign," and it deals with our sense of self and our general temperament when people first meet us. You will often hear this referred to as "the mask we wear in the world." I'm not a huge fan of that reference, as it implies that our ascendant is a "facade" of sorts. That's not true. Our rising signs are a big part of who we are. It just happens to be the parts of ourselves that we've learned are the most comfortable for us to put out into the world before people get to know the other parts of us. The 1st House also deals with our physical appearance. There are lots of cool things to look into in terms of physical features on the human body as linked to various rising signs. Give it a Google. It's fun.

We experience 1st House profection years at ages 0, 12, 24, 36, 48, 60, 72, 84, and 96. During these years, our focus shifts to our bodies and reconnecting with our sense of identity. You can look to the ruler of your 1st House and where it sits in your chart. For instance, I'm a Virgo Rising. So, my 1st house ruler is Mercury. Mercury sits in my 8th House. So, a 1st House profection year for me would be a blend of 1st and 8th House themes. You can also look to transits through those houses for additional information on themes that might arise during a profection year.

Lastly, the planets are the "doers" in a chart. So, when we see a chart with many planets in the 1st House, It indicates that the person focuses quite a bit of energy on their sense of self. Planets in the 1st House can also clue us into crucial parts of a person's identity. They tend to link to "identifier" adjectives when we're describing someone. For instance, let's say someone has Mercury (the planet of communication) in the 1st House. This person is likely to be very talkative and communicative. It would be something that would be a notable aspect of their personality. If you were describing that person to someone who didn't know them, you might say, "Oh, they're super chatty!"

TAROT (IRL)
ARIES - THE EMPEROR

Some of the organizing themes you'll see in various renditions of the Emperor card are deserts and the number four. Deserts are associated with the element of fire, and 4's deal with structure and stability. The Emperor is one of the most universally misunderstood cards in the deck. Looking at older descriptions for this archetype, we'll see words like "establishment" and "authority," and I think this is a big reason that many people have trouble connecting with it personally or even relating it to the Aries archetype.

Those words make the archetype seem rigid and stuffy, which isn't how we typically think about Aries. The central theme with the Emperor is how we carve out and permit ourselves to take up space in the world. That does require a sense of authority and establishing ourselves. But, we also have to remind ourselves that society informs everything we think, and when we remove the idea of gender, we start to progress in terms of the archetype. None of the cards are gendered, but because many decks often depict the Emperor as a man, there can be a tendency to default to looking at this card through a "masculine lens." This can make the card feel falsely patriarchal in many ways, which can alienate people. But, the fact remains that these archetypes are independent of gender.

Instead, what if we think about the general courage it takes to carve out and defend a space for ourselves in the world. That's the Aries archetype in the Emperor. It's the boldness and bravery that are alive in all of us. It's the stuff in our guts that says, "I built this structure. This space is mine. I'm going to occupy it wildly and without shame." That's the essence of the Emperor. On the Aries ("me"), Libra ("we") axis, when we take up space authentically, we become examples and space holders for others.

14

MARS - THE TOWER

And now...for one of the most universally feared cards in the deck, The Tower. This is Mars' card. Mars gives us the energy to create our "Tower" and also the power to destroy it.

Sometimes we build the structures that we think will keep us safe, but nothing is forever. As we evolve and change, sometimes we outgrow our "Tower," but that doesn't mean we aren't attached to it somehow. That's the work of this card. It's the universe coming along and removing something that we wouldn't ordinarily let go of without a push. The Tower feels unexpected, but that's just a part of Mars energy. It's spontaneous. It knows that when it's time, it's time.

People very rarely like the feeling of having "the rug ripped out from under them." However, think about all the significant changes in your life. There's a strong chance that they started with a "Tower Moment." This is where the considerable personal growth happens. These are divorces, deaths, major career shifts. It's the stuff that we just know, deep in our bones, is inevitable or isn't working, but we don't know how to let go. So, Mars assists us in the process. It's not here to cause hurt or harm for hurt or harm's sake. It's here to clear space so that we can rebuild something that's better for us in the place of what once was.

The Star follows the Tower in the Major Arcana. These difficult "Tower" moments are followed by moments of profound clarity and rejuvenation. Honestly, the Tower is here FOR us. It's one of the hardest working cards in the deck. So, when you see the Tower, resist the urge to resist. This card is here to honor the cycle of creation and destruction. Everything that lives will die. Everything that is built will crumble. We cannot truly grasp the concepts of gratitude and happiness without understanding loss and sadness. We also can't take the risks associated with moving forward unless we crumble parts of our past and present.

THE PAGE OF WANDS - CARDINAL FIRE

Who is the Page of Wands? This Page is loosely aligned with Cardinal Fire energy. They're a fire and earth combo. It's childlike. They feel young, fresh, and inexperienced - creatively passionate, yet still in the process of getting a grasp on the earthly aspects of their craft.

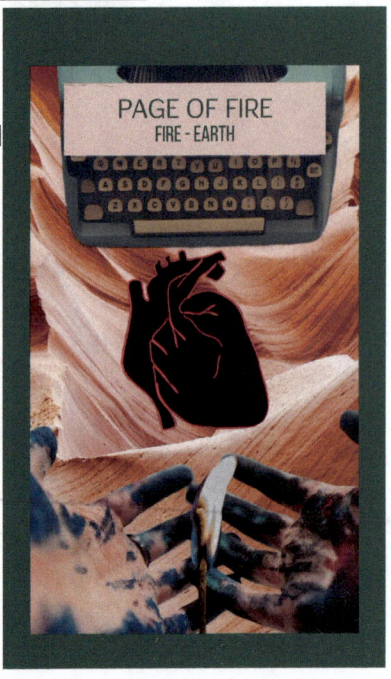

This is someone brimming with fresh enthusiasm, although likely without much real-life experience. The Page of Wands comes through in those moments in life when we're swept up in the excitement of something new without truly understanding the practical aspects of what the thing needs in order to be sustainable.

Think back to being a child. Remember the eagerness and elation to experience it all? Remember the wonder you felt at all the newness in the world around you? That's the beauty of this archetype. It's playful and naive. On the one hand, sometimes we need to feel these bursts of energy to "get us going" in life. Often, we can be so afraid of risk that we plan ourselves to death, when what we really need to do is just jump into the thing that we're excited about and learn as we go. Sometimes, this is where the genius happens, and we nail it on the first try. That's the magick of Cardinal Fire Energy, baby!

But, on the other hand, this archetype's downfall can be not looking before leaping. Along with the magick of adolescence, we also get scraped knees, broken bones, and bruises when we're not careful. There's an aspect of experimenting with limits in this archetype, much like children do when they're trying to find their footing in the world.

So, when you're in the Page of Wands, feel that excitement. Soak it in. But also, remember that what you have in enthusiasm, you may lack in experience.

THE KING OF WANDS - CARDINAL FIRE

The King of Wands is aligned with Cardinal Fire energy in the court. The King of Wands is mature fire - fire on fire. This archetype is the pioneer, the innovator. But, where some of the other fiery court cards can fizzle with time, the King of Wands knows how to harness the power of fire and sustain the burn. It's mature, wise, elder energy. This King knows how to simultaneously be the spark of change and also the sustainer of change.

When we're in King of Wands space, we exude warmth and confidence, and we have the skills to facilitate the mission at hand. This card comes through in those moments in life when we've done the thing we set out to do. It's self-possession. We took a leap towards a thing we wanted deep in our bones, we trusted our instincts, we worked hard, and we achieved what we set out to accomplish.

This King is the natural born leader in all of us. They exist to create a container for something bigger than themselves. In this way, they're very entrepreneurial in nature. They are fueled by a creativity that is outside the pre-established societal boundaries, and yet, they inherently understand that they have to work within a system to change the system. There's a maturity here that knows how to use the tools and existing structures to their advantage towards a larger goal.

But, this King isn't all business. There's a warm and inspirational quality to them. They're approachable. They understand human connection and how to ignite the fire within others. This King is simultaneously creator and steward, activist and organizer, engineer and builder.

One watch-out for this king: When we're in King of Wands space, with so much fiery energy, we have to be careful not to destroy the thing we're trying to build.

MEET THE COURT (IRL)
MEET THE PAGE AND KING OF WANDS (IRL)

Use the camera on your phone to scan the QR code and access blogs where we'll discuss real life examples of the Page and King of Wands.

ARIES SEASON TAROT + JOURNALING PROMPTS
ASK THE EMPEROR...

These prompts are perfect for Aries Season tarot inquiries or even as journaling prompts. If there's one thing fiery Mars/Aries energy does well, it's candidness. So, be honest with yourself here. That's really the way to get the most out of the season.

HOW COMFORTABLE AM I WITH TAKING UP SPACE?

WHAT DO I REALLY WANT RIGHT NOW?

WHAT STAGNANT ENERGY REQUIRES CLEARING?

HOW AM I INVITED TO GET IN TOUCH WITH MY ANGER?

WHAT IS SOMETHING I'M EXCITED ABOUT?

AM I BEING THE MOST AUTHENTIC VERSION OF MYSELF?

ACE OF WANDS - CARDINAL FIRE

INSPIRATION - POTENTIAL ENERGY - CREATIVE SPARK

When we're in this Ace, we're experiencing the spark of something new. This is kind of like the universe saying, "Hey, you know that thing you've been thinking about doing? Just do it already." The directive here is to pursue our passion, whatever that may be. The universe is telling us that the option is on the table, and we can do with it what we will.

The thing to remember here is that Aces represent potential. This doesn't guarantee results. We are still required to put in the work to do the thing. This card represents those initial stages of manifestation work where we're identifying what we would like to manifest. But, the real meat of this type of work is action-based. We are bombarded with opportunities and potential every single day. It's the fact that we select an opportunity and shift that potential energy into kinetic energy that actually gets us the thing we're after.

2 OF WANDS - MARS IN ARIES

PLANNING - INITIATIVE - DECISIVENESS

We were presented with opportunity in the Cardinal Fire Energy of the Ace of Wands. In the 2, we've made the conscious decision to turn that potential energy into kinetic energy. All of the 2's in the deck deal with decision-making and balance to some degree or another, and the Mars/Aries combo in this card showcases the bold decisiveness that is their hallmark. It's in the 2 of Wands that we've made our decision to act, and we start to make realistic plans for how to get to our future state.

It's important to note that the 2 of Wands is sort of an "in-between" space. We're mentally prepared for our future state, and we're definitely making plans for how to go about pursuing it. But, we haven't started truly actioning it just yet. We're still very much in our familiar, present state. This card is an invitation to get our "ducks in a row," so that we're ready when it's time to move.

3 OF WANDS - SUN IN ARIES

PURSUIT - ACTION - EXPANSION

We got our spark of inspiration in the Ace of Wands, and we did our planning, under the Mars/Aries influence of the 2 of Wands. Now, in the 3 of Wands, we're embodying sun in Aries energy. We're finally actioning this opportunity, and we're opened up for further opportunities and expansion.

The 3 of Wands always feels like a card that's got a little dual energy. There's the aspect of the card that's the pursuit, where we're actually going after the thing we want. But, there's also an aspect of this archetype where a longer-term future vision is now in view. So, in a lot of ways, it lives in both the present and the future simultaneously. This is where we start to think bigger. We start to wonder what this thing can become. It's not rooted in a toxic, capitalistic place. It's purer than that. This is divinely-inspired expansion.

4 OF WANDS - VENUS IN ARIES

CELEBRATION - HOMECOMING - APPRECIATION

We spoke about the significance of the number 4 when we talked about the Emperor. Fours represent structure and stability. When we layer in the Venus influence (comfy, home-y, harmonious vibes) alongside the Aries influence (energetic and warm), we have a recipe for a big homecoming celebration. This is a moment to appreciate everything we've done from the Ace through the 4, all that planning and hard work and expansion. It's a reminder to not forget where we come from. There is often an element of "home" associated with this card (whatever "home" means to us, individually, of course).

When we're in 4 of Wands space, we've accomplished something and we're returning home to our loved ones to share in joy and celebration. We have to remember to savor these moments.

TOXIC POSITIVITY
WHEN DID HEALTHY RAGE BECOME A CRIME?

Countless memes on the internet might have you believe that every Aries you know is just an angry little baby, running around yelling at everything. Aries is sort of known for its legendary temper. Now, I'm not saying being angry all the time is great, but there's also a really big problem right now with toxic positivity in the modern spiritual community.

Anger and frustration are natural human emotions, and there's a lot to be learned about ourselves in these spaces. Psychologists are catching on, with many arguing that being positive has become a new form of moral correctness. Emotions are a package deal. We don't get happiness without sadness. We don't get joy without rage, and there's a lot to be learned from our anger.

Anger work centers around the idea that our emotions tune us in to our value systems. Specifically, when we experience an uncomfortable emotion, such as rage or sadness. What that emotion is telling us is that something in our lives is out of sync with our personal value system.

For example, let's say something unfair happened at work, and we feel angry. That signals that justice and fairness are important to us. It's a super simple concept, but where it gets a little more complicated is how we choose to action the information we're uncovering and processing. So, let's keep with that same example. We now have a choice to action this thing we've noticed. Maybe we decide to confront the issue to bring more of a sense of justice to our workplace. Maybe we decide it's time for a new job that's more aligned with our values.

The point is, anger serves a purpose. It helps us identify what really matters to us, and we can only action what we acknowledge. Toxic positivity robs people of this kind of autonomy. So, before you tease Aries for their temper, just remember, experiencing the full spectrum of emotions and giving yourself permission to action them is true emotional intelligence. Now, let's get you in touch with your rage and value system this Aries Season...

RAGE JOURNALING 101
WHY YOU MAD?

Anger and frustration are part of teaching us about our value system, but they're also responsible for pushing us. We've all heard the stories about the person who, when flooded with adrenaline, can lift a car to save someone from danger.

When we get angry, our sympathetic nervous system becomes triggered. This system is responsible for directing our body's rapid involuntary response to threats - real or perceived. We all know what this feels like. Our hearts race, and our muscles tighten. Our blood pressure increases as adrenal glands flood our body with adrenaline. In these moments, we can become capable of things we wouldn't ordinarily be able to do, and that's something worth exploring.

Below, you'll find some prompts for keeping a rage journal. The prompts are more for when you're reflecting on anger while not directly under its influence. However, when you're feeling angry or frustrated, if you have the presence of mind, journal it out. Release everything. You don't need a prompt for that. It doesn't have to be neat or pretty, but it does have to be honest. It's always interesting to reflect back on how we perceive our anger from the outside versus when we're "in it." Clear themes may also present themselves over time. This helps us better understand our triggers and our values.

- **WHEN IS THE LAST TIME YOU WERE ANGRY? WHY WERE YOU ANGRY?**
- **WHAT IS THE MOST ANGER YOU'VE EVER FELT? CAN YOU PUT YOURSELF BACK IN THAT HEADSPACE? DESCRIBE IT.**
- **WHAT ARE THE 5 THINGS THAT ANNOY YOU MOST? IS THERE A THEME?**
- **IF YOUR ANGER HAD A COLOR, SMELL, TASTE, AND/OR SOUND, WHAT WOULD IT BE?**

KITCHEN WITCHIN'
SHE SPICY

Aries energy is bright and fresh and, of course, spicy. This homemade salsa recipe checks all of those boxes and is super quick and simple to throw together!

INGREDIENTS

- 1/4 white onion, coarsely chopped
- 1 garlic clove
- 1 lb roma tomatoes (cut into large chunks)
- 1 jalapeno pepper (seeds removed, optional)
- 1/4 cup cilantro
- Juice and zest of 1 lime
- 1/2 tsp sea salt
- 1/4 tsp cumin
- pinch of sugar

INSTRUCTIONS

1) Add the coarsely chopped onion and garlic to a food processor and process until they're well-chopped.
2) Add all of the rest of the ingredients and pulse until combined. The texture should be chunky, so be careful not to over-process. The spice level can be adjusted by adding more or less pepper, to taste. Leaving the seeds in will also up the spice.
3) You can strain some of the liquid if you find the salsa to be too watery. This varies based on the water content of the tomatoes.
4) Store any leftover salsa in an airtight container in the fridge for up to 3 days.

PRACTICAL MAGICK
LET YOUR INNER ARIES BABY COLOR IT OUT

Adult coloring books are having a moment right now, and for good reason! This childhood pastime has been shown to offer a number of mental health benefits including stress reduction and improved vision, motor skills, sleep, and focus. So, let your inner child out for a while, and wind down with some Aries-Season-Themed coloring! Scan the QR code below to access the PDF, which is either printable (if you're old school) or compatible to be used for coloring on a tablet or any other mobile device.

ARIES SEASON COLORING

Use your phone's camera to scan the QR code & access this content.

ARIES SEASON WORDS: THE TAKEAWAY
TAKE UP SPACE

So many of us are societally conditioned to make ourselves small, to shrink ourselves for the comfort of others. The seasonal energy asks us to own our space and stand up for ourselves, even when it means choosing the more difficult path or doing something uncomfortable. In short, sometimes being nice is overrated, and if we didn't advocate for ourselves, we wouldn't be able to count on anyone else to do it on our behalf. Aries energy is self-reliant and self-focused, for better or worse.

But it's not about aggression all the time. Sure, this energy is excellent at standing up for something, and it certainly doesn't back down from a fight. But, there's also an earnest quality at play. There's a high premium placed upon discovering and embodying the most authentic version of who we are (1st House themes at work). So, what you see is very much what you get. There's rarely an ulterior motive. The archetype is like a puppy - intensely loyal, pure in intent, and playful (albeit a little on the rough or clumsy side).

The season's energy is also focused on being willing to take risks (within reason, of course). I know the idea of making bold moves isn't comfy for all of us. But, hey, the old saying "fortune favors the bold" didn't just appear out of nowhere. We live in a world where no risk often means no reward. This is a period tied to re-emergence and action. It's physical. It's not a time for pontificating. It's a time for doing.

It's also the season of primal intuition. This is different from water sign intuition. These are the carnal parts of us. It's animalistic. It understands the thrill and necessity of the hunt and that carving out a space for ourselves in the world is essential to our survival.

Don't be afraid of your passion, excitement, boldness, or rage in Aries Season. It all serves a purpose.

Lastly, I'm a Pisces Mercury, and I communicate best in "vibes," vignettes, music, and art. So, we'll wrap each section with some words that capture the imagery and feeling of the archetypes...because it's just how my brain works.

ARIES
An eager hand raised -
> I know the answer. (No, I don't know how. I just know I know, ok?)

Screeching tires -
> Who needs red lights? (We have places to be.)

Restless brains and legs in bed -
> Don't you ever get excited about tomorrow? (Just me?)

Eyerolls -
> Why are people so fake? (Just say wtf you mean.)

The thrill of the chase -
> Better than sex. (Well, maybe...)

A heartbeat racing -
> It's just not fair. (I know, I know...life's not fair.)

The heat of a pepper -
> It hurts, but why do I want more? (Dopamine release.)

A toddler's tantrum -
> The way it feels to be told no. (Every cell in my body says yes.)

Brass knuckles -
> Because they look cool. (I wish you would.)

Spring break -
> Shots. (Fuck it. No rules tonight.)

Resignation email -
> Life's too short for bullshit jobs. (And no one tells me what to do.)

Runner's high -
> A body alive with endorphins. (Pavlovian response.)

Truth or Dare?
> Dare. (Always dare.)

Screaming a song in my car -
> Why are we so concerned with "inside voices?" (What a silly concept.)

Open windows -
> Who knew winter air had an expiration date? (Out with the old...)

Big plans -
> I can do anything I set my mind to. (Watch me.)

Tactless -
> A meat dress on the red carpet. Public Beef. ("I don't know her...")

What are you so afraid of?
> Literally nothing. (And absolutely everything.)

25

TAURUS

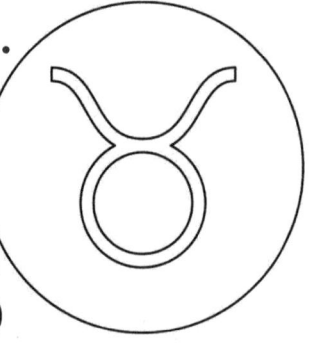

- **DATES: APRIL 20 - MAY 20**
- **ELEMENT: EARTH**
- **MODALITY: FIXED**
- **RULING PLANET: VENUS**
- **HOUSE: SECOND**
- **PHRASE: I HAVE**
- **GLYPH: THE BULL**
- **TAROT CARDS: 5 OF PENTACLES, 6 OF PENTACLES, 7 OF PENTACLES, QUEEN OF PENTACLES, THE EMPRESS, AND THE HIEROPHANT**

TAURUS SEASON PLAYLIST

USE THE CAMERA APP ON YOUR PHONE TO ACCESS THIS PLAYLIST.

TAURUS - A BRIEF INTRODUCTION

Aries Season kicked off the astrological new year and got us started with a bang! It's the responsibility of the cardinal signs to initiate their respective seasons, but they aren't the modality that is responsible for seeing the energy of the season through.

That duty is assigned to our fixed signs. The Cardinal Fire of Aries can be intense, but it's what's required to "wake everything up" for Spring. Now, the Fixed Earth energy of Taurus comes along and asks us to slow down and "root ourselves" into the season. The fixed signs are slow-moving, hard-working, and unwavering. In Taurus, the ideas from Aries season are brought to fruition. We move at a much more measured pace, which is required to sustain the season's mission.

In Taurus Season, the weather is getting warmer. It's time to plant seeds. It's time for fertilization. It's time for new growth. Taurus is known for both its "green thumb" and its patience. Growing things take time! Also, with regards to the earlier fertilization reference, many people think that the Taurus glyph (the circle with the horns shown on the opposite page) represents a bull's head and horns. But, historically, this glyph was meant to represent a uterus and fallopian tubes as a symbol of Spring's fertility. Although to be fair, the glyph works as a bull's head too...

Taurus is known for is its slower-moving nature, and it has everything to do with how the archetype processes information. Taurus energy is the embodiment of "be here now." It's a sensual sign, and what I mean by that is that it experiences life most fully through the five senses. It's critical for Taurus to taste, see, smell, hear, and touch the world to understand it completely. People often misunderstand Taurus' love of food, music, comfort, and beautiful things as generally self-indulgent behavior, but it's a meditation in true mindfulness. It's all about being completely present and sponging up the pleasure in every situation. Taurus energy is that of the tactile learner. These are the folks who learn by touching and doing.

Taurus Season is a time for a deep appreciation for all the tangible and worldly things we enjoy in this life. So, sink into an elaborate bath, put on your comfiest pajamas, grab a snack, kick back, relax, and let's soak up some Taurus Season Vibes!

TAURUS (IRL)

Taurus Season offers us an opportunity to stabilize. This is our chance to steady ourselves after the big bang that was Aries season. Taurus energy is deeply grounded. In Taurus season, we dig into the work. It's about the real deal, down-to-earth stuff that just needs to get done. The bull is often a sign of strength and persistence, but bulls also enjoy a good graze and nap in the sun. As much as Taurus is known for being a hard worker, it also embodies the latter.

One of the major Taurus stereotypes is that it can be a bit self-indulgent or even lazy (when it's in one of its more restful periods). But, what we see here is Taurus as a master of energy conservation. Remember, it isn't all grazing in the fields for bulls. They also charge! Taurus has a keen ability to conserve energy for when it is genuinely needed. It understands that to muster the stamina required for the methodical and tenacious work so characteristic of Taurus season, they must also rest and partake in the activities that allow them to relax and recharge. Being so grounded in the body and the earthly realm, with Taurus, it isn't just about the work that the body can do. It's also about all of the pleasure the body can enjoy.

The other major Taurus stereotype is that of being stubborn. Taurus works hard for what it has, and the Fixed Earth nature of the sign knows precisely what it wants. Once Taurus makes up its mind or sets its gaze on something, little to nothing can be done to sway them. They are nearly impervious to outside influence.

So, how do we use all of this information about the Taurus archetype to our advantage in real life? Taurus season is a fabulous time to stay committed. If you started a project in Aries Season or just generally have a project going that you've been struggling to commit to, Taurus season is the time to buckle down and put in the work. It's also an excellent time for setting personal boundaries. Use that natural Taurus stubbornness to your advantage! Lastly, it's a great time to be in our bodies. By that, I mean: get an expensive haircut, go for a massage, buy the handbag you've been drooling over, makeover your bed with fresh and luxurious bedding, enjoy a super over-the-top bath, cook yourself your favorite meal from scratch, and savor it. It's all about working hard and healthy hedonism for Taurus Season.

MEET VENUS

We know Venus as the planet of love, beauty, pleasure, and things of value. Venus has dual rulership or stewardship over Taurus and Libra. The more tangible, earthly aspects of Venus typically get linked up with Taurus, and the love and relationship parts of Venus usually get connected with Libra. So, for this section of the book, we'll be covering the earthly, tangible aspects as they relate to Taurus, and we'll cover the other half of Venus' domain in the Libra section.

Venus has a 225-day orbit, which means that we typically get one Venus Return per calendar year, but sometimes we can get up to three (if Venus is retrograde). So it's not like our birthday. This means it won't fall on the same day each year, but we will get at least one per year.

So, what does a Venus Return do? When Venus swings around to its spot on our natal chart annually, it works (in a Taurus sense) to set the tone for our relationship to money, things of beauty, and earthly possessions over the next year. Some astrologers suggest we look to the day before and after our Venus Returns. Paying particular attention to what happens on those days clues us into what Venus has in store for us for the year.

Venus is traditionally associated with money. While that's not entirely incorrect, I would argue that a modern definition of Venus is a bit broader. As it relates to Taurus, Venus helps us clarify our relationship to what we value and what we enjoy with our five senses. It's the music we can't get enough of, the art we love, our favorite food, and yes…our relationship to money and tangible material wealth.

Our Venus sign and house placement clue us into what we deem valuable, how we enjoy earthly pleasures, ways in which we might find creative fulfillment, and our sense of personal taste and aesthetic.

But Venus isn't all decadent snacks and naps. In the material sense, the trouble with Venus is that it often has a hard time distinguishing between what is a want and what is a need. As a result, there can be a tendency towards over-indulgence when Venus goes a bit out of balance. Venus isn't logical. It's emotional. So, when we're heavily under Venus' influence, it's important to remember to enjoy ourselves, but also to keep ourselves in check.

IT'S JUST A PHASE...
TAURUS SEASON MOONS (IRL)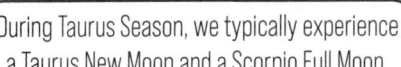

> During Taurus Season, we typically experience a Taurus New Moon and a Scorpio Full Moon.

TAURUS NEW MOON

The Taurus/Scorpio polar axis deals with themes of resources, both material (Taurus) and shared or non-material (Scorpio). New moons are typically a time for fresh starts. Taurus is focused on comfort and luxury. When we are in a Taurus New Moon, it's a great time to slow our pace and do something relaxing with our hands. Plant something, cook and enjoy an elaborate meal, or drink a tea that's good for the throat or thyroid. Taurus rules the throat, after all. Taurus New Moons are also a fabulous time to take a pause and get your finances in order if that's something that you struggle with. Balance your bank account, create a budget, and start a savings plan to begin working with. Taurus has a serious need for security, and this is a great time to get honest with yourself about how well you're planning for your future.

SCORPIO FULL MOON

The Scorpio full moon provides a bit of counter-balance in Taurus Season. It reminds us that money, luxury, and security aren't everything. After all, you can't take it with you when you die. Full moons are typically a time of wrapping things up and preparing for release. Scorpio is the sign of death and rebirth. Its goal is to help us discern truth and determine what's really important. There's refining energy to Scorpio. Taurus is all about the practical. It's all about the here and now in terms of earthly and tangible things. The Scorpio full moon comes as an emotionally intense flipside to the Taurus energy to shake things up a little. Its goal is to strip away and release the things that are no longer working for us. In short, more isn't always more. It's just like Mase said, "Mo Money, Mo Problems." The Scorpio Full Moon is a great time to break bad habits and purge things that no longer meet our needs. This leaves space for new things, our continual evolution, and rebirth. Nothing is meant to stay the same forever, and the Scorpio Full Moon is an ideal time to come to terms with that and create space for what's next. So, purge away!

WELCOME HOME
THE 2ND HOUSE (IRL) - THE HOUSE OF VALUE

In a natural chart, Taurus is associated with the 2nd House, and it's often referred to as the "House of Money." However, I prefer "House of Value" since the 2nd House is about much more than just money. The 2nd House deals with themes of resources and resource management. Debt can also live in this house and the polar house (the 8th House). The 2nd House also rules over our possessions. But, there's a lot more to this house. As humans, we often use material possessions to define ourselves. The car we drive, our clothing, and our belongings, in general, say a lot to the world about who we are. So, in some ways, it could be argued that we use our 2nd House identity to convey who we are to the world and attract specific people and situations into our lives.

The planets are the "doers" in a chart. So, when we see a chart with many planets in the 2nd House, we have someone dedicating quite a bit of their energy to the material world. It signifies that it's part of their "blueprint" to be grounded in the earthly realm. They'd be concerned with exploring experiences on the physical plane. The sign on the cusp of the 2nd House also gives us clues as to how people prefer to accrue and manage their resources. For instance, if someone has Libra on the 2nd House cusp, we might see someone who amasses their wealth, possessions, and sense of self-worth via their relationships with others. This would be someone who likely places a lot of importance on their partnerships. There can also be a very balanced and generous quality with Libra on the 2nd House cusp.

Outside of natal planets in the 2nd House, transits to our 2nd House and 2nd House profection years help us continually evolve and refine how we deal with value. These transits also reveal changes to our money, material possessions, and even our self-esteem and sense of general security. We experience 2nd House profection years at ages 1, 13, 25, 37, 49, 61, 73, 85, and 97. As always, we can look to the ruler of the sign on the 2nd House cusp, it's placement in the chart, and relevant transits for more specific information around what a specific profection year holds for us. Take a look at your 2nd House. Based on what's there, what would you say you value? What does it tell you about how you prefer to manage your resources?

TAROT (IRL)
TAURUS - THE HIEROPHANT

Taurus is associated with The Hierophant in the Major Arcana. Historically, before the general population was literate, Hierophants were responsible for interpreting and sharing sacred texts with the public. The Hierophant deals with themes of institutions, spirituality, and rules.

More traditional definitions of the card will say that The Hierophant is all about learning from trusted and established sources. This archetype has a lot to do with how we engage with the systems and institutions all around us.

Sometimes we are absolutely the student in this card, but I like to think of The Hierophant as how we can become our own teacher in a more modern sense. It represents how we can re-shape the establishments around us for lasting change (very "fixed" Taurus vibes).

It's important to remember that we think of the student and teacher dynamic as hierarchical. When, in truth, it's much more cyclical. We all learn from one another. We're perpetually students. Throughout our lives, we're like little sponges. We soak up all the information from the world around us. These can be things that our parents have taught us, ideas or habits we picked up from teachers and peers in our adolescence, or even concepts we've been taught through the religions we may have been raised in.

The Hierophant comes along when we need to ask ourselves what is true for us. These are the periods in our lives where we get to decide how we want to re-write the rules for ourselves. While Hierophant periods can be incredibly fruitful in learning to live our unique truth, that's not to say that they aren't complicated. There can be some severe isolation that comes with redefining things, but as with any change, however uncomfortable, it's usually for the best.

VENUS - THE EMPRESS

Venus, Taurus' ruler, is associated with the Empress in the Major Arcana. This card gets gendered pretty aggressively in a lot of tarot writing. Traditional definitions say this card is about "feminine energy" and "motherhood." What about those people who aren't or can't be mothers. What about people who don't identify as women? All of the tarot is for all of us. So, what's the central theme here? What's the part of this archetype that universally applies to all of us? It's an invitation to receive.

It's a card about all those Venusian themes: abundance, openness, and creativity. It's about being a nurturer. We can be nurturers to pets, children, creative projects, businesses, any number of things.

So, when we distill it back, what's really at the center of this card is the idea of being open to receiving what's for us in the universe and taking the necessary steps to care for those things. Sure, it sounds lovely and amazing. Who doesn't want abundance and creativity, right? But think about how difficult it can be to receive things in real life without feelings of guilt or shame. Can you think of a time when someone paid you a compliment, and it made you feel awkward? There is often a feeling that we don't deserve these things, and that's the essential lesson of The Empress. This card is here to teach us that we all deserve to receive. We all deserve abundance by our own definition.

So, when we're in an Empress space, we're being invited to open up. We have to allow those opportunities into our lives, and that's often easier said than done. I know it has a lot to do with the conditioning of Western Capitalism, the idea that we have to work for everything we have and that we're not "entitled" to anything. But this card isn't about entitlement in a negative sense of the word. It's about knowing that we're worthy and deserve to enjoy happiness and abundance in our time on this planet.

THE QUEEN OF PENTACLES - FIXED EARTH

Who is the Queen of Pentacles? This Queen is aligned with Fixed Earth energy. They're a water and earth combo, elementally speaking. Queens represent mature, stable, adult energy, typically with internal focus. The Queen of Pentacles feels like "home" in many ways. This Queen has an almost inherent understanding of comfort, but that's not to say that they're not willing to put in the work for the things they want. Like Taurus Energy, this Queen works hard and relaxes hard, and understands that all the best things take time. This is the stuff that's worth the wait.

This queen has mastered mellow, nurturing energy. Their finances are in order. They have a green thumb. They rival Martha Stewart in their ability to cook and entertain. They have all the patience in the world and possess an effortless grace.

When we're in a Queen of Pentacles space, we're invited to take care of ourselves and those around us, and let's be honest...self-care is more extensive than taking a fancy bath. I mean, this Queen can get down with a luxurious bath too...but only after their work is done. In reality, self-care also means hard work to ensure long-term security and stability for ourselves and our loved ones. This means ensuring our finances, homes, and jobs are in order. This Queen is also an invitation to be present in the moment. They understand how to enjoy life as it's happening, and when we pull this Queen, we're being invited to do the same.

So, when this Queen shows up, stop and smell the roses, make a meal from scratch, invite some friends over for dinner, remind yourself that slow and steady wins the race, and don't forget to balance your checkbook.

MEET THE COURT (IRL)
MEET THE QUEEN OF PENTACLES (IRL)

 Use the camera on your phone to scan the QR code and access blogs where we'll discuss real life examples of the Queen of Pentacles.

THE MINOR ARCANA

5 OF PENTACLES - MERCURY IN TAURUS

NEED - LACK - WORRY

All of the 5's in the deck are a bit contractive, and the 5 of Pentacles is no exception. We all know the feeling of 5 of Pentacles. It's the times when we're living on ramen, the bank account is in the red, we're steeped in worry, and we just don't know how we're going to keep on keeping on.

I'd be lying if I said that 5 of Pentacles space felt great. It typically doesn't. However, there's a lot to be learned in this space. These are the times that humble us. Sure, our self-esteem and ego may take a hit when we're hanging out with this five, but the good news is, it's a member of the Minor Arcana. This means the period is typically short-lived, and this too shall pass.

The big lesson with this 5 (along with staying humble) is that once we're back on solid ground again, we can look back and remember what this period felt like. Hopefully, this helps us remember to be generous to others in need.

35

6 OF PENTACLES - MOON IN TAURUS

GENEROSITY - SYMBIOSIS - GIVING

Coming out of our period of scarcity in the 5 of Pentacles, we now have a keen understanding of need. In the 6 of Pentacles, we're being reminded of the symbiosis that applies to everything that exists on the planet. To receive, we have to give freely. We offer what we have when we can, and we take what we need in times of scarcity. Capitalism is rooted in individualism, and sometimes we forget this basic truth. Humans are social creatures, and we need community.

Giving isn't always financial. In the 6 of Pentacles, we can also give our time and energy, or even our advice and wisdom to someone in need. This card encompasses the interconnectedness of everything. In many ways, it can feel like a mini version of The Wheel of Fortune (at least in an earthly sense). The Wheel of Fortune holds the secrets to the natural balance of things, and the 6 of Pentacles very much keeps a similar balance.

7 OF PENTACLES - SATURN IN TAURUS

INVESTMENT - PERSEVERANCE - PACING

Having learned lessons around need and generosity in the 5 of Pentacles and 6 of Pentacles, the 7 of Pentacles teaches us to play the long game for our stability and security.

This card is all about learning lessons around the proper investment of our time and resources for delayed gratification. This involves adequate pacing and knowing that rest is required as a part of perseverance.

It teaches us about putting in the slow and measured work, fully understanding that the rewards will not be instantaneous. This isn't a get-rich-quick scheme. We're building something sustainable here, and if we are to go the distance, we have to learn lessons in patience, planning, and pace. But, it's all worth it in the end with the 7 of Pentacles.

PRACTICAL MAGICK
GET INDULGENT FOR TAURUS SEASON

As we've already established, Taurus loves a little luxury and also the opportunity to work with its hands to make something tangible. So, give this DIY ritual bath recipe a whirl. Put on your favorite playlist (if you're at a loss there, we provided a QR Code to a pre-curated Taurus Season Playlist at the beginning of this section), prepare your favorite beverage, light a candle, and grab your favorite reading material.

DIY TAURUS RITUAL BATH

Use your phone's camera to scan the QR code & access this bonus content.

TAURUS SEASON TAROT + JOURNALING PROMPTS
ASK THE EMPRESS + THE HIEROPHANT

These prompts are perfect for Taurus Season tarot or even as journaling prompts.

WHAT AM I BEING INVITED TO RECEIVE IN THIS MOMENT?

WHAT AM I BEING INVITED TO NURTURE IN THIS MOMENT?

WHERE/HOW DO I HOLD LIMITING BELIEFS AROUND WHAT I DESERVE? WHAT SELF-CARE COULD I USE RIGHT NOW?

WHAT IS SOMETHING I'VE BEEN TAUGHT THAT NO LONGER RESONATES WITH ME?

WHAT IS TRUE FOR ME? AM I ACTIVELY LIVING IT?

KITCHEN WITCHIN'
CARB-Y COMFORT FOOD

Taurus loves a good carb-y treat, and let's be real...everything tastes better with butter. Gnocchi is Italian comfort food. It's made from a remarkably simple list of ingredients, but the magick is in the love and time taken to prepare it from scratch. The recipe quantities below serve four.

HOMEMADE RICOTTA GNOCCHI WITH LEMON BUTTER SAUCE

INGREDIENTS
- 2 cups ricotta cheese
- 1/2 cup freshly grated parmesan
- 3 egg yolks
- Large handful of finely chopped chives
- 2 large handfuls of finely chopped Italian Parsley, separated
- 1 pinch nutmeg
- 1 tbsp sea salt
- 1 1/2 cups flour
- 6 tbsp unsalted butter
- Juice of 1 lemon

INSTRUCTIONS

1) In a large bowl, combine the ricotta, parmesan cheese, egg yolks, one handful of chopped Italian Parsley, one handful of chopped chives, nutmeg, and salt. Gradually mix in the flour. A soft dough will begin to form. Be sure not to over mix it.

2) Flour a surface and divide the dough into fist-sized pieces. Roughly roll into 2 cm thick strings. Slice each string into 2 cm pieces, and dust with a little extra flour.

3) Place the prepared dough pieces in the fridge to chill for roughly a half hour before cooking.

4) Heat butter in a pan, add lemon juice, the other handful of chopped Italian Parsley. Salt and pepper to taste. Set aside.

5) Salt and boil water, and add the gnocchi. Boil until they float to the top. Use a straining spoon or slotted spoon to move the gnocchi into the pan with the prepared sauce, and gently mix. Ladle into shallow bowls and garnish with more Italian parsley and parmesan cheese.

SAY THANKS
HOW BEING THANKFUL CHANGES OUR BRAINS

We've talked a lot about how Taurus has a healthy love of "stuff," but what's the point of having a bunch of stuff if we don't appreciate it? There's a basic principle in economics called Diminishing Marginal Utility. Essentially, the concept says that past a certain point of meeting our basic needs, accruing more and more material wealth brings us less and less joy.

Enter the trend of gratitude journaling. When we consciously focus on what we have and the privileges we enjoy, it changes our brains. Study after study has shown that a regular gratitude journaling practice supports a wide range of health benefits, including improved sleep quality and mood, reduced levels of anxiety and depression, less fatigue and inflammation, and reduced risk of heart failure. So, enjoy all of the sensual pleasures of Taurus Season to the fullest, and try incorporating a regular gratitude journaling practice as well. Check out the prompts below for some inspiration.

WRITE DOWN SOMETHING YOU ACCOMPLISHED TODAY AND HOW YOU FEEL NOW THAT IT'S COMPLETE.

DESCRIBE YOUR FAVORITE PART OF THE DAY.

WHAT FRIENDS AND FAMILY MEMBERS ARE YOU MOST GRATEFUL FOR? WHAT TRAITS DO YOU ADMIRE IN THEM?

WHO OR WHAT IN YOUR LIFE ARE YOU HAPPY TO HAVE LET GO OF? HOW HAS IT IMPROVED YOUR LIFE?

LIST 3 PEOPLE OR THINGS YOU TAKE FOR GRANTED. HOW CAN YOU SHOW MORE APPRECIATION FOR THEM?

TAURUS SEASON WORDS: THE TAKEAWAY
PACE YOURSELF + TREAT YOURSELF

Call it what you want ("hustle culture", "grind culture"), but capitalism has us collectively feeling like if we're not hyper-productive every second of every day, then we're not worthy. Conversely, the ultra-aggressive counter-movement for indulgent "self-care" can swing the pendulum too far in the opposite direction. It often ignores the privilege that self-care requires, and the fact is, humans need to work. We need a purpose. Taurus energy is about the balance between these two extremes, which is where we would ideally be existing. The season reminds us that sustainable work towards a goal requires pacing and time for rest.

Taurus energy is also about exploring the things we can enjoy with our five senses. We exist on a physical plane, and part of that experience is tangible. Part of being human is to observe beautiful things, eat good food, and feel comfort in our bodies. Taurus energy teaches us about being truly present in our little flesh-prisons - big Empress energy.

It also teaches us that kinesthetic learning is valid. Sometimes we need to experience something to learn it. This is how we build personal value systems that we can stand behind - big Hierophant energy. For example, we often hear about Taurus being "stubborn" and inflexible. Yes, that's a thing. All stereotypes are rooted in some truth, but the "why" behind them matters. Under Taurus' influence, when we adopt a stance, we have taken the time and lived experience to form a belief we can be firm in. This is why it takes so much effort to convince Taurus energy to be open to a change.

This is a season for slow and steady work towards a goal, and it's also a season to prioritize downtime and enjoyment. We're learning about the intricacies of healthy work/life balance under the Taurus archetype. Self-care looks different for everyone, and this is a conversation that we need to be having. For some, it can be purchasing a designer bag. For others, it might be binging a TV show while meal-prepping for the week. There is no right or wrong answer here. It's just the little things we do to unwind and make our lives a bit more manageable.

So, find your stride, and work hard during Taurus Season, but also, remember to reward yourself for a job well done (within your means, of course). Otherwise, what's the fucking point?

TAURUS

Roots clinging to dirt -
>The plant equivalent of heels dug in. (You will not move me.)

A metronome clicks -
>Tick, tick. (Where's your sense of rhythm?)

Perfectly-plated meal -
>It's almost too pretty to eat. (Almost...)

The jingle of layered jewelry -
>What's the point of owning it if you don't actually wear it? (YOLO.)

A bank account in the green -
>One day the thing will be yours, kid. (Just keep at it.)

Siesta -
>Why are naps reserved for children? (They don't even have jobs.)

Rhythmic breathing -
>It's a marathon, not a sprint. (Something about a tortoise and a hare?)

Familiar couch and mattress craters -
>Sink and release. (This is all yours.)

A cow in a field -
>Lounging and grazing... (Energy stores have to be built up, you know?)

A bull charging -
>Potential energy turned kinetic. (But, only for the really important stuff.)

A mirage of expensive toiletries -
>Because you're worth it. (Duh.)

Closely held convictions -
>I lived it. I touched. I felt it. (That's how I know.)

A dog guarding a bone -
>It's mine. Get your own. (Growl.)

Admiring your gallery wall -
>More is more. (Bitch, you've got taste.)

Perfect buttery latticed pie crust -
>What's the point if it's not going to be decadent (...and beautiful)?

Fashionably late -
>I don't wake up looking this, you know? (I'll get there when I get there.)

Sun on skin -
>Sit. Lay. Soak it in. (Vitamin D, baby.)

Opulence -
>Enjoy it while you're here. (You can't take it with you when you die.)

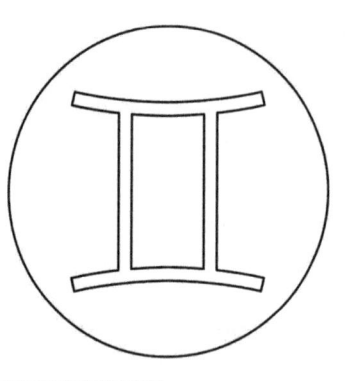

GEMINI

- **DATES:** MAY 21 - JUNE 20
- **ELEMENT:** AIR
- **MODALITY:** MUTABLE
- **RULING PLANET:** MERCURY
- **HOUSE:** THIRD
- **PHRASE:** I THINK
- **GLYPH:** THE TWINS
- **TAROT CARDS:** 8 OF SWORDS, 9 OF SWORDS, 10 OF SWORDS, KNIGHT OF SWORDS, THE LOVERS, AND THE MAGICIAN

GEMINI SEASON PLAYLIST

USE THE CAMERA APP ON YOUR PHONE TO ACCESS THIS PLAYLIST.

GEMINI - A BRIEF INTRODUCTION

Taurus Season was about planting seeds and putting down roots. It was a time for slow, steady work and enjoying sensory pleasures. As we enter Gemini Season, the hard work is done. The days are warmer and gradually growing longer. We have time on our hands as we wait for what was planted in Taurus Season to grow. Finally, the Summer Solstice is approaching. Nature is putting on a spectacular display, and we spend our time outside socializing and exchanging ideas.

Gemini represents Mutable Air energy. All of our mutable signs are tasked with the job of change. They're here to prepare us all for the seasonal shifts. We can sense that we're in the last days of mild weather and transitioning from spring to summer. We're moving from the focus and determination of Fixed Earth energy in Taurus into more adaptable and go-with-the-flow Gemini energy. The Taurus to Gemini Season shift also broadly represents a change from being rooted in our bodies sensually to spending more time in our minds. It's a shift to the cerebral.

When the sun is in Gemini, our collective antennae go up. Our minds become electric with curiosity. I like to think of Gemini energy like that of little nerve synapses. We're picking up information, digesting it, sorting it, and sharing it. Communication becomes paramount, and we're hungry for ideas in all their varied forms. We become bored more easily. We multi-task.

During Gemini season, our schedules fill with fun gatherings. There are loads of options for getting out in the world and spending time with people. There are festivals, cook-outs, and pool parties, which is perfect for Gemini, our social butterfly of the zodiac.

In terms of solo activities, this is also an excellent time for Mercury-friendly activities that pique our curiosity and keep our minds busy, such as reading, writing, watching documentaries, and listening to music or podcasts.

So, ready all your best anecdotes, indulge your curiosities, and get ready to socialize! It's Gemini Season!

GEMINI (IRL)

We can't talk about Gemini without recognizing that it's one of the most widely roasted signs on the internet. Two-faced, scatter-brained, and high-strung...you can't throw a social media stone without hitting an astro meme detailing all the reasons why Gemini's are "just the worst." But is that even true? A deeper look at the Gemini archetype reveals that these lower octave stereotypes are not entirely founded.

If you have even a rudimentary understanding of astrology, then you've no doubt heard the cliches which universally regard Gemini as conniving and addicted to gossip. Hot take: that's bullshit. The root of this stereotype is that Gemini is dual in nature, but that doesn't necessarily equate to being two-faced. What I find to be more true of Gemini is utilizing that duality to examine ideas from all sides. I think of it as a form of "intellectual empathy." Gemini can "try on" the thought patterns of others. There's a unique penchant for objectivity and openness to viewpoints that aren't it's own. It can detach it's emotions and look at an idea in a multi-faceted way for exactly what it is. This makes it relational. When you talk to a Gemini, it's like you can sense them tracking with your train of thought. They know what it is to truly engage.

You'll be hard-pressed to find a better person to share a conversation with. Period. The exchange of ideas is paramount for Gemini. It's great at taking in vast expanses of information, processing, making connections, and disseminating it in a useful way. Gemini is knowledgeable enough for lively discussion and debate, possessing unparalleled wit and coupled with the fact that it knows a little about everything and everything about nothing. Still, it remains curious enough to avoid the dreaded "know-it-all" syndrome.

I'm not sure how we landed in a place where certain zodiac signs are demonized by default, but I'd love to offer up some alternative descriptors for Gemini. They're not high-strung. They're cerebral and curious. They're not chatterboxes. They're conversationalists. They're not two-faced. They're open-minded and flexible. As astrology becomes a more significant part of popular culture, I hope we can collectively lay some of these zodiac stereotypes to rest because they're seriously tired.

MEET MERCURY

Gemini shares quick-moving Mercury as a planetary ruler or steward with Virgo. Mercury is the closest planet to the sun and has a tight, fast orbit of 88 days. In mythology, Mercury is portrayed as the messenger god. It naturally follows that Mercury deals with themes of communication, commerce, transportation, short-distance travel, our brain chemistry, and our analytical abilities. Where Mercury falls in our natal charts says a lot about how we think and communicate.

With such a short orbit, we typically get one Mercury Return a year around the time of our birthday, although it's not usually on the same day. Mercury Returns help to refine and develop our sense of personal expression. They also help to clue us in on how we'll be spending our mental energy for the year to come.

We can't talk about Mercury without talking about Mercury Retrograde. All planets have retrograde periods, but we experience several Mercury Retrograde periods each year because of Mercury's short orbit. As a result, people tend to be most familiar with them. Also, meme culture and pop culture astrology have blown the effects of Mercury Retrograde way out of proportion.

First, let's get some facts straight. Retrograde periods occur when a planet appears to move backward in the sky from Earth's vantage point. These planets are not actually moving backward. From a physics perspective, that wouldn't be possible. The best example is to imagine that you're driving on a highway and a semi-truck pulls up in the lane next to you. If the semi-truck were to accelerate further and your speed didn't change, the truck would pull ahead, and your car would appear to be moving backward. But, of course, you're both still moving forward. It's just an optical illusion. In essence, this is what's happening when planets go through retrograde periods.

It's even more important to mention that retrograde periods are not a thing to be feared. These are merely periods for "re" words. We should be using the time to review, revise, reflect, and rework. Mercury retrograde is preceded by a roughly two-week-long shadow period which helps us adjust to the slowdown, and it's also followed by an approximately two-week shadow period which allows us to integrate the lessons learned. So if you need to sign contracts or travel, don't panic. It's totally fine. Just make sure you review everything thoroughly.

IT'S JUST A PHASE...
GEMINI SEASON MOONS (IRL)

During Gemini Season, we typically experience a Gemini New Moon and a Sagittarius Full Moon.

GEMINI NEW MOON

The Gemini/Sagittarius polar axis deals with themes of locality and processing information, but the signs differ in their preferred scale. Gemini prefers dealing with the local community and zeroing in on nitty-gritty details, while Sagittarius favors expansive travel to distant places and big picture thinking. I think of Gemini energy almost like a microscope and Sagittarius energy as observing great expanses from the vantage point of an airplane. Keeping that in mind, Gemini New Moons are periods of pause used for listening, noticing, and absorbing information that's in our immediate surroundings for inspiration. Spend some time observing your immediate surroundings and really listening to the people around you. Get curious. Sometimes our most valuable sources of inspiration are right in front of our faces, and we don't even realize it.

SAGITTARIUS FULL MOON

After a waxing moon period in Gemini Season, we experience a Sagittarius full moon. Part of how we absorb information is intellectual, but part of it is also intuitive. This full moon reminds us to balance the intellectual busyness we experience in Gemini Season with more intuitive, big picture Sagittarius themes. Let your feelings and your gut guide you during Sagittarius Full Moons. It's a great time to think about the big picture. Are there books, music, art, or other media that you're drawn to during this time? If so, go with it. Indulge in whatever you're being pulled to. You don't have to have all the answers right away regarding what to "do" with the information, questions, or feelings it brings up in you. You have time to reflect on that. You might even like to make a list or a journal entry about it. Revisit it during the next full moon in the grounded and practical Capricorn full moon and see if you've been able to decode any of the information.

WELCOME HOME
THE 3RD HOUSE (IRL) - THE HOUSE OF COMMUNICATION

Shocking no one, the 3rd House deals with Mercurial themes such as communication and our thought processes. We can look to the sign on the house cusp and any planets found within the house to clue us in on the specifics of what that might look like on a person-to-person basis.

The 3rd House also speaks to short-distance travel, local community activities, and our relationships with siblings, classmates, and coworkers.

This house describes how we analyze problems. It tells us about our learning style, how we like to research, and how we perceive information. The sign on the 3rd House cusp acts a lot like having Mercury in that same sign. For example, if someone has Pisces on the 3rd House cusp, it behaves similarly to Mercury in Pisces. This person might learn through absorption. They may know things and not know how or why they know them. They can be prone to picking up information without ever being conscious of it.

A big part of how we communicate is described by what's happening in the 3rd House. It speaks to our preferred mode of communication and our comfort level with public speaking, writing, and broadcast. It can also say a lot about specific artistic abilities, specifically music and dance.

This house also represents our earliest independent childhood experiences. While our childhood family and "roots" are more of a 4th House thing, the 3rd House describes how we experience school as children. It says a lot about our childhood friendships and our relationships with our siblings if we have them. We also learn about relating to our local community in the 3rd House. People with lots of planets in the 3rd House might have a lot of focus, connection, and influence locally.

We experience 3rd House profection years at ages 2, 14, 26, 38, 50, 62, 74, 86, and 98. As always, we can look to the ruler of the sign on the 3rd House cusp, its placement in the chart, and relevant transits for more specific information around what a particular profection year holds for us. Take a look at your 3rd House. What does it say about your sense of curiosity and communication?

TAROT (IRL)
GEMINI - THE LOVERS

There's a common misconception that pulling The Lovers equates to a romantic relationship on the horizon. While that can be a thing, more often, what we see in The Lovers is an invitation to examine the dual nature that's present within all of us. It's one of the more complex cards in the Majors, and it deals with themes of self-love. It's about seeing all the lovable and admirable parts of ourselves through the lens of a third party. In the Lovers, we're seeing others' perceptions of us reflected back at us. Most Lovers card imagery features artwork with themes highlighting duality, symmetry, and mirroring.

This card asks us to honor the fact that humans are complicated. I'm going to age myself here, but it reminds me of the Meredith Brooks song "Bitch." We're all "a little bit of everything; all rolled into one." We get to be both saints and sinners, silly and serious, all at the same time.

At its center, The Lovers is all about options and choice. On the one hand, this archetype is about unifying dual but equal forces. On the other hand, it's about being in touch with ourselves enough to make the choices that are most in alignment with our values. The Lovers follows the Hierophant, so it only makes sense that we're building upon that work.

When we're in Lover's space, we're learning how to fully love and accept all facets of ourselves. Self-love is prerequisite work to begin being fully present in our relationships with friends, family, and romantic partners. We have to learn to be honest with ourselves about the many facets of who we are and offer ourselves compassion and acceptance. So, yes, the Lovers is about unity, harmony, and love, but not always in the way we might think.

MERCURY - THE MAGICIAN

The Magician is Mercury's card in the Major Arcana. Mercury has dual-rulership or stewardship over Gemini and Virgo. So, there are aspects of this card that align with both the Virgo and Gemini archetypes.

We typically see all four suits of the Minor Arcana pictured on the card, as well as a hand pointing up and a hand pointing down.

The suits of the minor arcana (pentacles, swords, wands, and cups) represent the four elements (earth, air, fire, and water, respectively). These are the creative tools at our disposal. The hand pointing up and the hand pointing down represent universal inspiration channeling through us into the things we create here on the physical plane.

The Gemini side of the archetype is communication with the universe. It's airy. These are those "lightning bolt" moments where we get a jolt of inspiration for something. The one-word descriptors that come to mind for this card are "out" and "through." The word "through" represents the Gemini side of the Mercurial energy of the card. We are a vessel for what the universe wants to communicate or bring to life.

The word "out" represents the Virgo side of The Magician. This is the part of the Magician archetype that's focused on the act of creating. It's earthy. We're using the tools at our disposal to create something tangible and universally inspired to put out into the world.

Pulling the Magician is a message that we have all the necessary tools for the task at hand. It's a time to create something real and magickal. It's associated with new beginnings, opportunities, and tapping into our full potential towards manifesting a divinely-inspired future for ourselves.

THE KNIGHT OF SWORDS - MUTABLE AIR

All of the knights in the court describe qualities of movement. When we're embodying the Knight of Swords, we're moving quickly and directly, propelled by our intellect. This is one of the fasted moving court cards in the tarot.

Knights represent teen/adolescent energy, which is exciting but can also be inexperienced. The Mutable Air energy implies opportunities for rapid change, and this archetype represents those moments in life when our mission is clear, and we have laser focus. This knight is assertive and quick to act. When we're in the Knight of Swords space, our mind is set on a goal, and there's little to nothing that can stand in our way.

Since this archetype is so dynamic, its energy is difficult to sustain for extended periods. This knight tends to show up for us when we need to use a calculated burst of energy to achieve a particular goal, but if we experience it for more than a short period, we can become prone to burnout and nervous tension.

This energy feels a lot like cramming for finals at the end of a semester. We're temporarily driven by purpose, and the rhythm of "normal life" is disturbed. Priority is given to the task at hand, and the things we would usually be doing to keep ourselves balanced take a back seat. However, it's not intended to be our forever state.

Sometimes life demands this kind of focus, especially if we're to capitalize on the opportunities that present themselves. The key to this court card is knowing when to lean into it and when to return to a more sustainable pace. Now, go get 'em'!

MEET THE COURT (IRL)
MEET THE KNIGHT OF SWORDS (IRL)

Use the camera on your phone to scan the QR code and access blogs where we'll discuss real life examples of the Knight of Swords.

---

8 OF SWORDS - JUPITER IN GEMINI

SELF-VICTIMIZATION - POWERLESSNESS

I'm not here to tell you that the swords are the comfiest suit in the minor arcana. That would be a lie. But, I stand by the fact that they are a suit that works incredibly hard for us. Brains are complicated, and so are the swords.

The 8 of Swords speaks to the mind as a prison. This card represents those times in our lives when we think that we're trapped. The keyword here is "think." It's totally self-imposed. We may believe we are at the mercy of something outside of ourselves, but the truth is, we're the limiting factor. We're restricting ourselves.

When we find ourselves in the 8 of Swords' territory, it's a good time to do work in reclaiming our personal sense of power.

51

9 OF SWORDS - MARS IN GEMINI

ANXIETY - NIGHTMARES - WORRY

As an insomniac who struggles with Generalized Anxiety Disorders, I feel the 9 of Swords in my body and bones on, like, a cellular level. I also have my natal Mars in Gemini. So, this card has a special place in my heart.

Are you losing a ton of sleep, trapped by negative thoughts, feeling anxious? Is your mind spinning out on things that you know aren't actually problems? Welcome to the 9 of Swords, and here's your complimentary shot of cortisol.

Here's the thing, Gemini is widely associated with mental agility, which is generally super helpful. However, when in excess, it also has the capacity to manifest as anxiety and hypervigilance. So when you find yourself here, it's time to take care of a frazzled nervous system, however that may look for you. And for the love of god, get some rest!

10 OF SWORDS - SUN IN GEMINI

END OF A CYCLE - DEATH OF A TOXIC PATTERN

Ok, so the 10 of Swords is a pretty gnarly-looking card in most decks, and I'm not going to pretend that it's comfy. It's not. But, as with any prickly card, it's here to help us with some big, heavy stuff.

It's about the death of old and toxic thought patterns. In the 10 of Swords, we recognize that what we're doing isn't working. Change doesn't happen when things are comfortable, and change itself isn't always comfortable. But, it is a necessary part of life and our growth as humans.

These are the "breakthroughs" we have in talk therapy or the moments where we realize we're imitating a toxic pattern we learned from a parent and we make a conscious decision to change. They're not always pretty moments, and they don't come without work and self-awareness. But, they are a welcome and necessary new beginning towards something better.

PRACTICAL MAGICK
A MERCURY RETROGRADE EXERCISE TO GET YOU IN TOUCH WITH PAST VERSIONS OF YOURSELF

This simple exercise is perfect during Mercury Retrograde periods when we are asked to slow down, review, and reflect. If we're willing to document the details, there's a lot to be learned from the past version of ourselves.

By now, you've likely gathered that there is a lot of archetype overlay in tarot, astrology, and numerology. So, this is an exercise dedicated to understanding how those archetypes look for you throughout your life.

We're aiming to examine the Gemini/Sagittarius polarity. Remember, the organizing theme for their shared axis is around scope and granularity. Gemini likes to get in the weeds, and Sagittarius loves the big picture. So, we're going to get into the nitty-gritty details on an annual level and then zoom out and look at the big picture for the unique journey to where we are now.

You can format this however feels most natural for you. Some people prefer to make a table. Others prefer to do this in prose, journal-entry style.

Start with the year that you were born, and compile for each year:
- Your age
- What profection year you were in that year (There's a reference table in the front of the book with that information.)
- Any planetary returns you had that year (You can use any free planetary return calculator online to get this information.)
- What your annual tarot cards for that year were (These are calculated by adding the individual digits of your birthday and the year in question, reducing to number(s) 21 or less, and correlating it to the major arcana. For example, my birthday is April 9th. So, my 2021 birth cards are calculated by adding 4+9+2+0+2+1, which equals 18. So, 2021 would be a Moon Card year for me. Also, 18 can be further reduced, 1+8=9. Therefore, it would also be a Hermit year for me. You can have one card or more than one card for each year.)
- If you can pull photos from those years, they're super helpful to bring to the exercise. It helps with visualizing and remembering, but it's optional.

Now, the important part, what do you remember most about the year in question?

Sit with the granularity. Try to remember what each year felt like for you. Then, "zoom out." Look at the larger cycles at play.

- Review the themes of all of your 1st and 12th House profection years together. These represent our Jupiter Return cycles. Jupiter cycles are responsible for expanding us and personal growth. You can look at all your 2nd House profection years together to get a sense of financial/tangible cycles, or 3rd House profection years for examining larger cycles and growth in curiosity and communication, so on and so forth.
- Look at your Saturn Return cycle(s) if you're old enough to have had them. Saturn Returns mark the thresholds through the major phases of the human life cycle.
- Calculate your tarot life card. (This is calculated the same way as the tarot year card, the year is just subbed out for your birth year, and we typically reduce to a single digit. Most people only use one card for this.) This card represents the central theme you're here to learn about in this life. How in alignment are your larger cycles with this main theme?

This is a great exercise to add to and to reflect on during retrograde cycles with each passing year.

GEMINI SEASON TAROT + JOURNALING PROMPTS
ASK THE LOVERS + THE MAGICIAN

These prompts are perfect for Gemini Season tarot or even as journaling prompts.

WHAT AM I OVER-ANALYZING? HOW CAN I KEEP MYSELF GROUNDED IN MY BODY?

HOW CAN I BEST EXPRESS MYSELF IN THIS MOMENT? WHAT CAN I CREATE?

WHAT SUPPORT MIGHT I FIND IN MY LOCAL COMMUNITY?

WHAT DUALITIES ARE ALIVE WITHIN ME? HOW DO I RECONCILE THEM?

GEMINI SEASON JOURNALING
HOW "THE 5 WHYS" HELP US DIG DEEPER

Is there any sign more curious than Gemini? In my time working as an engineer, I spent a lot of time problem-solving. One of the troubleshooting methodologies we frequently used was "The Five Whys."

The basic premise is that we often assume we know the root cause of something, but what we think is at the root of the issue is just a symptom of a deeper underlying root cause. So, we continue to ask a chain of five whys, with each one bringing us closer to the root.

We start with a problem statement, and we ask ourselves why that is. Then, once we have that answer in statement form, we ask why again until we've asked why five times. Well, I guess technically, it can be more or less than five times, but the idea is that you ask until you can't answer anymore. Then, where you land will typically be the root cause.

Take one of the problem statements below, complete it, and journal through the five whys or come up with one of your own. Challenge yourself to see how deep you can go. This exercise can be a valuable investigation into what makes us tick.

1) My biggest self-sabotaging behavior is _____.

2) _____ make(s) me angrier than anything in the world.

3) _____ is my most closely held belief.

4) I'm most afraid of _____.

5) I feel most vulnerable when _____.

6) I feel most motivated when _____.

7) _____ makes me feel appreciated.

KITCHEN WITCHIN'
TWO-FACED (SWEET + SPICY)

Gemini season wouldn't be complete without a shareable dish that reflects its signature dual nature. These cauliflower "wings" are incredibly simple to throw together. They're also a crowd favorite for parties and other social gatherings or even to enjoy alone while reading a book or watching a good documentary. The quantities below yield four servings.

INSTRUCTIONS

1) Preheat the oven to 400 F, and line a baking sheet with parchment paper. Spray with olive oil cooking spray.

2) In a medium mixing bowl, beat the eggs and season with salt and pepper.

3) In a separate medium mixing bowl, combine your dry ingredients (breadcrumbs, flour, salt, and pepper).

4) Dip each piece of cauliflower in the eggs mixture and then in the breadcrumb mixture. Shake off any excess breading, and place each piece onto the baking sheet.

5) Bake for 25-30 minutes. While the cauliflower is baking, prepare the sauce.

6) Add the maple syrup, light brown sugar, soy sauce, garlic paste, ginger paste, and red chili paste to a small pot and whisk as you bring it to a boil. Reduce to a simmer and whisk for around 2 minutes. Then, remove from heat and allow the sauce to thicken as it cools.

7) When the cauliflower is done baking, combine the cauliflower and sauce in a large bowl. Shake the bowl a bit to make sure the pieces are coated in the sauce. Garnish with toasted sesame seed and chives and serve!

INGREDIENTS
- 1 medium head of cauliflower (cored and cut into florets)
- 2 large eggs
- 1 cup breadcrumbs of your choosing (I like panko)
- 3 tbsp all-purpose flour
- 4 tbsp maple syrup
- 2 tbsp light brown sugar
- 1 tbsp soy sauce
- 1 tsp garlic paste
- 1 tsp ginger paste
- 1 tsp red chili paste
- salt and pepper
- sesame seeds, toasted
- chives, finely chopped
- olive oil cooking spray

GEMINI SEASON WORDS: THE TAKEAWAY
I THINK. THEREFORE, I AM.

Gemini Season is a time for curiosity. We're mentally energized under Gemini's influence. It's an excellent time for multi-tasking and energizing our social lives leading up to the summer solstice at the start of Cancer Season. It's a time for connecting with others and communicating ideas. It's a time to allow mutable energy to wash over us so we can be open to the possibility of change.

Gemini dissects. It examines. When we're under the influence of some of the more emotionally-driven water or fire signs, our logic can be colored by instinct or emotion. The opposite is true in airy Gemini Season. Our emotions are processed through a cerebral filter. So it's a great time for reflection and understanding why we do the things we do. We've already established that Mercury Retrograde periods are significant for this kind of work.

It's about honoring our consciousness and the power of perception. Maybe this is why Gemini is so open to shifting viewpoints. It has an inherent understanding of the value of varying perspectives. Because I mean, not to get philosophical on you here, but the world only "exists" to us because we have the consciousness to perceive it. It's like Descartes said, "I think. Therefore, I am." Our consciousness is a magical thing.

Humans are complex. There's some terminology used when we look at aspects within birth charts. Some aspects are classified as "easy," and some as "hard." Those labels make it seems like easy aspects are "good" and hard aspects are "bad." But, really, easy aspects simply "work together," and hard aspects ask us to be more than one thing simultaneously, which requires a little work. I regularly tell clients that charts with lots of hard aspects make for very flexible and adaptable people. This feels like the essence of Gemini. It's kind of a Gemini superpower. Yes, it's busy. Yes, it can be confusing. Yes, there can undoubtedly be mental tension, but it's also adaptable and flexible.

The world is a big place with endless possibilities, and Gemini wants to process everything. So, let your curiosity run wild during Gemini Season. Be open to the viewpoints of others, the possibility of change, and embrace all the different versions of yourself. The Summer Solstice is on its way!

GEMINI

House of mirrors -
    Reflections on reflections. Which one is the real me? (Trick Question...)
Lightning strikes -
    Electrostatic discharge connecting ground and atmosphere. (Never in the same place twice.)
Cells in mitosis -
    Dividing and dividing under a microscope. (Endless possibilities.)
Apple's Marimba -
    Social butterfly. (Let's catch up!)
A report card -
    "Likes to talk a lot during class." Only when I'm bored...(which is always.)
Drum and Bass -
    174 BPM (When the bass drops, so do my worries.)
A lawyer argues their case -
    "Let's play devil's advocate for a minute..." (Let me convince you.)
A surface covered in post-its -
    Organized chaos. (There's a method to the madness, I promise.)
An inquisitive child -
    "Why do I have two eyes if I only see one thing?" (Good question.)
A toilet papered neighborhood -
    Pranks as a love language. (We only tease you because we like you.)
A spider -
    Limbs multi-tasking in eight directions. (String by string connected to form a cohesive web.)
Class Clown -
    Sure, detention sucks... (But their laughter is worth it.)
A moving truck -
    You know that they say... (The only constant in life is change.)
A shark swimming -
    A pen tapping on a table, restless legs bouncing underneath. (If we stop moving, we die.)
An interviewer conducting an interview -
    What's your worst fear? (Monotony.)

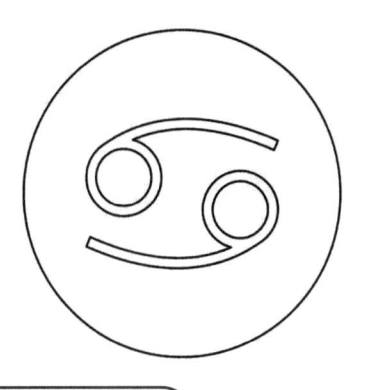

CANCER

- **DATES:** JUNE 21 - JULY 22
- **ELEMENT:** WATER
- **MODALITY:** FIXED
- **RULING PLANET:** THE MOON
- **HOUSE:** FOURTH
- **PHRASE:** I NURTURE
- **GLYPH:** THE CRAB
- **TAROT CARDS:** ACE OF CUPS, 2 OF CUPS, 3 OF CUPS, 4 OF CUPS, PAGE OF CUPS, KING OF CUPS, THE HIGH PRIESTESS, AND THE CHARIOT

CANCER SEASON PLAYLIST
USE THE CAMERA APP ON YOUR PHONE TO ACCESS THIS PLAYLIST.

CANCER - A BRIEF INTRODUCTION

Airy Gemini Season focuses us inside our heads. We spend time analyzing and multitasking. Cancer Season brings the Cardinal Water energy necessary to move us from our intellect directly into our feelings.

The Summer Solstice's days are long and hot, with the sun directly overhead. There's a collective need for water, a cooling down. Outside, it's lush and green as plant life ripens and water sources begin to dry. This is the time of year when the collective focuses on getting as much nourishment to food-producing plants as possible to maximize yields at harvest time. Likewise, it's critical to have enough food to sustain the population during the fall and winter months. These themes of nourishment and security are hallmarks of the Cancer archetype.

The Cancer/Capricorn polar axis deals with themes of stability. We're talking about tangible and earthly stability and security on the Capricorn side of things. With Cancer, we're looking at emotional stability and delving into family dynamics. We're exploring what feels like home to us. We're defining what makes us feel most cared for, how we care for those around us, and what provides us with a sense of ease and comfort.

Cancer energy is the feeling of being held by something. It's coming home after a long day at work and putting on your coziest pair of sweatpants. It's spending the entire weekend binging your favorite show or movie from the comfort of your couch. It's the smell of a signature dish, the recipe that you've loved since you were a kid. It's talking to an old friend or relative who always knows just the right thing to say.

The season is a great time to connect with yourself and explore themes related to support. Cancer is highly intuitive, and anything that helps get us in touch with our center is helpful. Lean into any reflective practices such as journaling or tarot. Use feelings wheels. Nourish your nervous system with a shower or a bath. Cook yourself some homemade comfort food.

But most importantly, this Cancer Season, be sure to ask yourself: What makes you feel most at home?

CANCER (IRL)

Astrological stereotypes might have us believe that Cancer is nothing more than a hypersensitive, extra emotional crybaby. Ruled by the ever-changing moon, there's undoubtedly a fluid quality to Cancer. Just as the moon changes phases, so do our feelings. However, the archetype isn't about being a passive victim of emotions that we have no control over. Instead, it's about consciously honoring and processing the full spectrum of emotional shifts we experience. Remember, Cancer is the crab. A rugged exterior protects it. So, the stereotypes that Cancer is shy and overly sensitive aren't always accurate. While soft and intuitive at its center, Cancer is more guarded than we might think. It doesn't spill its emotions to just anyone.

Crabs are also known for their side-stepping. Direct confrontation isn't typically one of Cancer's favorite things. But, when pushed, they will absolutely use those pinchers, especially if they are protecting themselves or a loved one. So, it makes sense that one of the big lessons of the season is discovering the balance between self-preservation and opening up to others.

Cancer is also universally regarded as a caretaker. Sure, many of us are human, pet, or plant parents, but Cancer Season reminds us that we can also parent ourselves. This is the time of year when we are afforded the intuitive ability to get clear on what we want out of life, the stuff that would bring us the most inner fulfillment.

So, yes, maybe we do experience heightened emotions during Cancer Season. But also, perhaps those emotions are "louder" during this time of the year so that we pay attention to what they're telling us. So, don't be afraid to explore your what they're communicating.

It comes as no surprise that we may feel called to hang out in our "crab shell" a bit more than usual during this time of year. Cancer is tied to our sense of home. This is supposed to be the place where we feel safe being vulnerable. We may prefer quiet time on our couch or intimate gatherings with the people we're closest to over being out socializing in large groups. These personal spaces create a container to hold all that watery Cancer energy. So, build yourself a cozy environment, and let your nervous system restore itself after busy a busy Gemini Season.

MEET THE MOON

The watery and changeable moon rules Cancer. This nighttime luminary has a quick orbit of only 27 days. Comprising one-third of our "big three," our moon placements are an essential part of our natal chart. The moon describes our emotional nature. It explains how we take care of others and how we like to be taken care of. The moon illuminates our private inner world and is a big part of defining our sense of home. We can also look to our moon placement for clues about our relationship with our parent who was the more prominent caretaker throughout our upbringing. We typically see the connection to our mother, but there are all kinds of family structures in the world. So, it can vary. Each month the moon moves through a series of phases. Not unlike the tide, there's a sort of an ebb and flow to the energy. Since the moon has a short, tight orbit, we experience a monthly lunar return.

The cycle starts with a new moon. New moons are a period of rest and clarity. They're a great time for self-reflection, course correction, and goal-setting. They carry the energy of new beginnings.

The waxing moon phase follows a new moon. This is the "busy" phase of the moon cycle. In this period, we start to create action around our goals. We're full of movement. We're exerting energy and expanding.

The full moon marks the middle of the cycle. There is a significant build-up of energy in the waxing moon phase until the moon is at its fullest. Full moons are a climax, so they can feel a bit intense. This is an excellent time for release and cleansing.

During the waning moon phase, the moon is getting darker again, moving from a full moon back to a new moon. So, it naturally follows that the waning moon phases are a time for slowing down, reflection, slowing down, and boundary work.

Eclipses occur during new moon and full moon periods, and they are linked to new beginnings and completion, respectively. Eclipses carry intense and often unpredictable energy. But, this kind of intensity is necessary, as eclipses are tasked with meaningful work. They powerfully illuminate our path. We experience moments of clarity and even redirection under eclipse energy.

IT'S JUST A PHASE...
CANCER SEASON MOONS (IRL)

> During Cancer Season, we typically experience a Cancer New Moon and a Capricorn Full Moon.

CANCER NEW MOON

The Cancer/Capricorn polarity deals with security themes, and new moons are typically a time for fresh starts. The Cancer side of the axis deals with themes of emotional security. So, it follows that we define what we desire in our home and family life under the Cancer New Moon. This is a great time to take inventory of your environment and relationships. What makes you feel most emotionally secure and supported? Are there close relationships that require work? How do you feel in your home environment? If anything feels off, now is the time to develop a plan for change. Our homes are our protective "crab shells." We should feel safe in our vulnerability there. This is where we recharge our batteries. So, get honest with yourself about what you need.

CAPRICORN FULL MOON

After spending the waxing moon phase getting cozy in our home environment, we get to experience some polar Capricorn energy at the Capricorn Full Moon. Full moons carry culminating energy and remind us of balance. Capricorn deals with tangible security and public image. We have access to structure in this period, shifting our focus to more practical endeavors. Under this full moon, we explore work/life balance, and we get a needed burst of productive energy. This full moon illuminates where we may have cut corners or missed details in the past. If we've become distracted from our goals, this full moon reminds us and gives us the push to get back in there and finish what we started. This period is excellent for getting clear on our public and career-related dreams, making plans, and getting organized. Get your schedule in order, and address broken and absent systems in your life that hold you back. Lastly, grounding ourselves is incredibly important when we're in any earthy full moon.

WELCOME HOME
THE 4TH HOUSE (IRL) - THE HOME + OUR ROOTS

The phrase "welcome home" takes on a new meaning when discussing the 4th House. The 4th House cusp is located at the very bottom of the natal chart. You will often see this point labeled as the nadir or Imum Coeli (IC for short), which translates to "bottom of the sky" in Latin. This house is tied to both Cancer and the moon. We experience 4th House profection years at ages 3, 15, 27, 39, 51, 63, 75, 87, and 99. As always, we can look to the ruler of the sign on the 4th House cusp, its placement in the chart, and relevant transits for more specific information around what a particular profection year holds for us.

The 4th House deals with our early family life, roots, and home (childhood and present-day). The zodiac sign on the 4th House cusp and any planets in the 4th House can shed light on our general attitudes around home and family. Along with our moon placement, this house speaks to how we perceive our relationship with our parents.

For example, if someone has Virgo on the 4th House cusp, their upbringing may have been quite structured, maybe even strict. As an adult, their home is likely neat and organized. Lots of folks with Virgo on this house cusp also work from home.

Something that's always interested me in understanding the 4th House is the linkage to the 10th House cusp, otherwise known as the Midheaven. When we get to the Capricorn section, we'll discuss the 10th House in more detail. But, it's important to note that the 10th House cusp is the highest and "most visible" point on the natal chart, and its cusp will be in the opposite sign of the 4th House. So, it makes sense that it deals with our public image, career, and reputation.

If the 4th House is where we come from, then it follows that the 10th House is where we're going. There will undoubtedly be behaviors and traditions that we pick up from our families of origin and carry on in the family structures we build for ourselves as adults. This is reflected in our 4th House placements. Alternately, we will experience things in our early home life that we will choose to do entirely differently. Those things are shown in our 10th House placements.

Take a look at your 4th house. What's home to you?

TAROT (IRL)
CANCER - THE CHARIOT

The Chariot is the 7th card in the Major Arcana and completes what many readers refer to as "Line 1" of the majors. When we line the majors up from 1 through 21 in increments of 7, we get three horizontal lines. The first line deals with our ego and establishing who we are. The second line deals with our interactions with others and our more profound connection to ourselves, and the third line deals with forces larger than us and the collective unconscious. The Chariot finishes line 1 and is the vehicle that moves us into line 2. We spend all of line 1 figuring out who we are and who we aren't, and then we get rapid movement and expansion into the world in The Chariot.

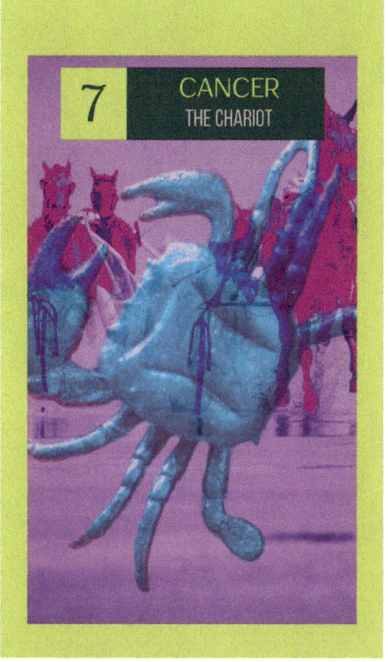

I liken the experience to a student going off to college or someone who has never left their tiny hometown traveling for the first time. It's rapid expansion. It's getting thrown into the deep end in the best way. So we're packing up our crab shell (Chariot) and traveling out into the great unknown for some new experiences.

While it may feel more like fire energy than water energy, remember, water isn't always still. Water moves, and water can move aggressively when it needs to (hurricanes, tsunamis). Cancer energy is Cardinal Water. It's initiating in nature and launches us into the intuitive realm. It feels like "tuning in" and getting a green light. When this card shows itself in a reading, it's time to move. It's time for action.

But, it's important to note that we can't stay in this energy for prolonged periods of time, or else we're prone to the worst kind of burnout. Sometimes that intense and intuitively-guided high level of activity and stamina are required to get us to where we're going, but there's no way we can sustain it long term.

MOON - THE HIGH PRIESTESS

The High Priestess is the Magician's counterpart. The Magician is focused on putting divinely inspired work out into the world. The High Priestess is about diving deeply inward. This archetype is all about accessing our inner power.

In 2016, a group of scientists found that our intuition is informed by experience. Meaning, we pick up tons of information consciously and unconsciously all the time, and we use it to extrapolate likely outcomes. Our brains utilize this information when making spontaneous decisions where data analysis isn't possible. The study showed that many of the same action-oriented brain neurons and pathways light up regardless of whether participants perform an action or watch someone else perform it. The observer's brain is acting out what it's witnessing. For instance, when a person sees a hand reaching for a glass, neurons and pathways activated by this system may help that person intuit the grasper's intentions.

We all have access to this instinctual decision-making ability. It's a part of being human. But, like any skill, we can strengthen our ability with practice, and if we don't use it, we can fall out of touch with it. The High Priestess is one of the cards people love until they receive it in a reading, especially when we're looking for clarity. The High Priestess shows up to say, "Why are you asking me? You already know the answer." And here's the thing, we do have the answer. We just have to listen to our gut. But, that doesn't make it any less frustrating when it shows up during a reading where we're looking for help with something that feels unclear. Most tarot cards invite us to action. The High Priestess calls for a pause, centering, listening, and feeling. As an archetype, there's a quiet knowing to this card. Maybe we're not listening to our instincts or have fallen out of our spiritual practice. The High Priestess shows up to remind us to jump back into it and reconnect.

THE PAGE OF CUPS - CARDINAL WATER

The Page of Cups is a water/earth blend of elemental energy. This page is all about inspiration in unexpected places and finding a fresh sense of play in our lives.

It represents a well of untapped creativity and emotion. Pages are youthful energy. Children are naturally creative because they haven't been pushed to be practical and sensible by society. They're also typically very trusting of others because they haven't yet learned that humans can have some pretty undesirable qualities, which can be useful or not, depending on the situation.

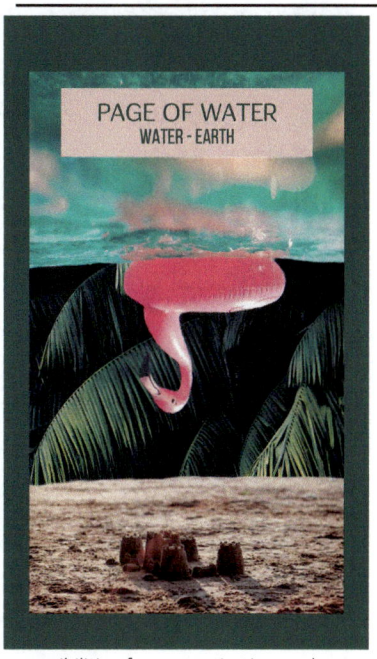

This card offers us the ability to see all the possibilities for recreation in our day-to-day activities and the ability to be open and trusting of those around us. On the flip side, this archetype can struggle to find its footing with a sense of responsibility. The pages are naive across the board. The Page of Cups wears rose-colored glasses (especially regarding relationships) and likely forgets when it's time to do their taxes. So when we're vibing with the Page of Cups, we have to be careful to enjoy ourselves, but also keep our heads out of the clouds.

When the Page of Cups shows up, it's time to look at our relationships from a fresh perspective. It can also indicate that we're about to get an unexpected wave of fresh creative inspiration. We're being asked to find amusement in the mundane and let our guard down. This archetype begs us to think outside of the box and to not be afraid to have some fun! It can be a welcome reminder that the universe has a sense of humor, and we shouldn't take ourselves too seriously.

In the Page of Cups, let yourself be light, and indulge your childlike sense of wonder. But keep your wits about you.

67

THE KING OF CUPS - CARDINAL WATER

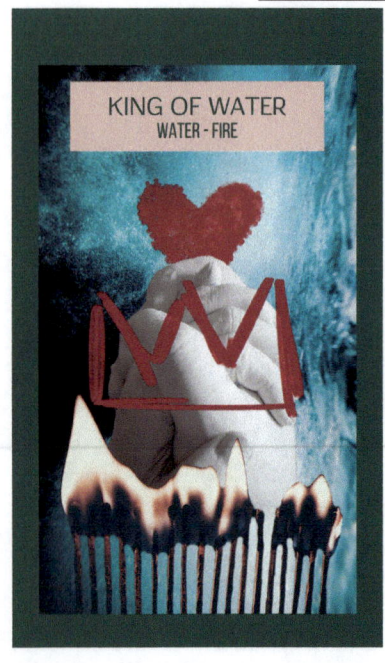

The King of Cups embodies emotional security and maturity. It's fire/water energy - big Fred Rogers vibes. It's deeply in touch with its intuition and feelings. It understands the importance of emotional boundaries and not getting swallowed up in our feelings.

Being emotionally mature doesn't mean we're always happy. That would just be toxic positivity and spiritual bypassing at work. Instead, it means that we know how to embrace the full spectrum of emotions. Yes, even the difficult ones. We know how to embrace joy and love in the King of Cups, but we also acknowledge and work with our anger and sadness in a healthy way.

This king understands the interconnectedness of everything, and as wonderfully woo as that all sounds, the world can also be a ruthless place. On the one hand, it's critical to connect deeply with the world around us. It's how we approach life with empathy. On the other hand, however, the world is also a wild place. If we gave ourselves over to experiencing and internalizing it without emotional boundaries, we would be wrecked all the time. This king represents generosity, devotion, and utilizing the proper balance between head and heart, thinking and feeling. It's tapped directly into the collective unconscious.

We're being called to a balanced approach in the King of Cups. This king is the compassionate advisor. Remember, Kings are wise, elder energy. It knows how to speak what we need to hear with a heaping side of empathy.

Don't be afraid to experience life heart-first in the King of Cups, but don't forget that all things are best in moderation. We can feel our feelings without being utterly consumed by them.

MEET THE COURT (IRL)
MEET THE PAGE OF CUPS AND THE KING OF CUPS (IRL)

Use the camera on your phone to scan the QR code and access blogs where we'll discuss real life examples of the Page and King of Cups.

ACE OF CUPS - CARDINAL WATER

FRESH EMOTIONAL ENERGY - NEW RELATIONSHIPS

All of the aces represent the simplistic essence of their respective suits. The cups connect us to the world of water, our inner realms, the subconscious, and our emotions. This ace represents a fresh emotional start, a clean slate.

This can look like new relationships, a reminder to connect with our intuition, a new facet of our spirituality to explore, or even a creative awakening.

This ace is an invitation to release the emotional baggage that restricts us. It's a signal that it's time to start fresh. This card often shows up after we've been through something burdensome. It's an indication that the tides are turning.

2 OF CUPS - VENUS IN CANCER

UNITY - PARTNERSHIP - MERGING

Alexa, play "I'll be There" by The Jackson 5.

Ok, but seriously, this card is like the younger sibling to The Lovers. It deals with themes of partnership and mutual respect.

When this card shows up for us, we're being asked to look at all the ways that partnership could be mutually beneficial. It's all about the magick that occurs when two forces work together in unity. This can be regarding romantic relationships, friendships, and business partnerships.

Like all the 2's, this card also deals with themes of balance, choice, and merging. So, this card can also show itself when we're being invited to evaluate our relationship to moderation.

3 OF CUPS - MERCURY IN CANCER

FRIENDSHIP - COMMUNITY - GATHERINGS

The 3 of Cups is about the short-lived moments of community and friendship that we all encounter in our lives.

This card always reminds me of the cast of a play or a band and crew on tour. A unique and temporary bond is formed in preparing and running a show like that. It's like a temporary family unit.

The 3 of Cups is also an indicator of reunions with long-lost friends and relatives. These are moments that deserve celebration.

When we're in the 3 of Cups, we're being invited to enjoy the here and now. Part of what makes these connections so special is that they're temporary. So, the 3 of Cups calls us to enjoy them while they last.

4 OF CUPS - MOON IN CANCER

APATHY - CONTEMPLATION - DISCONNECTEDNESS

From the Ace of Cups through the 3 of Cups, we're experiencing a lot of emotional expansion. We've moved through partnership and community, and now we're a little disenchanted. This card always reminds me of a stereotypical emo kid. You know the scenario, a brooding teen from the suburbs. They're presented with so many opportunities but choose to languish in their room wearing their signature dark eyeliner, of course.

This card represents periods where we have so much to be thankful for, but we find ourselves despondent and ungrateful.

The irony with this card is that the answers to the things that trouble us are abundantly available all around us. We're just choosing not to see them. But, hey, who am I to deny someone a good Taking Back Sunday binge every now and again?

CANCER SEASON TAROT + JOURNALING PROMPTS

ASK THE CHARIOT...

These prompts are perfect for Cancer Season tarot or even as journaling prompts.

WHAT JOURNEY AM I CURRENTLY ON?

WHAT'S THE STARTING POINT? WHAT AM I INVITED TO EXPLORE REGARDING MY ROOTS?

HOW DO I DEAL WITH CONFLICT OR BUMPS IN THE ROAD? WHAT IS MY TYPICAL GO-TO EMOTIONAL RESPONSE? WHY MIGHT THAT BE?

HOW WILL THE DESTINATION EXPAND ME?

CANCER SEASON JOURNALING
LET YOUR INNER HIGH PRIESTESS FREE-WRITE

Free-writing is an exercise that's been used for ages by writers and creatives. It helps tease out what's living in the unconscious mind. It entails writing continuously for a pre-determined period of time without any concern for grammar or spelling. The only rule is not to stop writing, no matter what. If you can't think of anything to write, just write that repeatedly until something comes to you. It should be full stream of consciousness. Don't force yourself into a particular topic. Simply let your mind flow. Wherever it leads you is totally fine.

The idea is to create a judgment-free container to capture whatever is living deep in our subconscious mind. Think of it as passing the mic to your inner High Priestess. The result likely won't be eloquent, but it may illuminate some themes for you to explore in a deeper capacity.

Take time to free-write daily. If possible, increase your duration gradually. Then, after a few weeks, take a look over your free writes. I bet you'll notice some recurring themes.

PRACTICAL MAGICK
DECORATE YOUR CRAB SHELL

Ever heard the term neuro-architecture? It's the study of how the human body and brain respond to built environments, which implies that the layout and decor in our surroundings affect our mental, emotional, and physical state.

Is there a better time of year than Cancer Season to get our homes in order? I don't think so. Re-decorating our home can help with everything from stress reduction to decision fatigue, and I think we could all use a little help with that...

Use the camera on your phone to scan the QR code and access some tips and tricks for making your crab shell your favorite place to be.

KITCHEN WITCHIN'
ITALIAN NUT ROLLS

For Cancer Season, I wanted to share a family recipe. These cookies were a staple at holidays and family gatherings when I was growing up. I don't even know if this is the actual "correct" name for them, but it's what we call them. My grandma would make a pot of coffee and put out plates of these whenever we visited. We would sit around the table and socialize while scarfing them down. They're sweet without being too sweet. Whenever I bake a batch, it's like walking into my grandma's house. The smell reminds me so much of "home."

INGREDIENTS

- 1 package active dry yeast
- 1/4 cup warm water
- 1 tsp sugar
- 1 cup butter, softened
- 2 cups all-purpose flour
- 3 egg yolks
- 1 cup sour cream
- 4 tsp vanilla extract, divided
- 4 cups walnuts
- 1 cup granulated sugar
- 1/2 cup milk

INSTRUCTIONS

- Combine water, yeast, and sugar in a bowl and leave for about 15 minutes to activate the yeast.
- Divide the butter into 4 equal parts in a large bowl, and add the activated yeast, egg yolks, sour cream, and 1 tsp of vanilla extract. Mix with a spatula.
- Place the dough in a glass bowl and cover with a dishtowel. Leave it to rest for at least 2 hours. You can leave it overnight if you like.
- Use a food processor to chop the walnuts into small pieces.
- In a separate bowl, combine walnuts, sugar, milk, and 3 tsp vanilla. Set aside.
- Preheat the oven to 375 degrees.
- Roll the dough to 1/8" thickness. The thinner you can roll the dough, the better.
- Cut the dough into roughly 3-inch squares.
- Put a heaping teaspoon of filling in the center of each square.
- Use a little bit of water to wet the edges of the pastry and fold two corners over the center of the filling to meet in the middle. It should look like a little tube with the nut filling sticking out a bit on each end.
- Place the rolled cookies on an ungreased baking sheet, and bake for 15 minutes.
- Optional: Some folks like to wait for these to cool and then sprinkle them with a little bit of powdered sugar. My grandma never did this, but I know lots of people who do.

CANCER SEASON WORDS: THE TAKEAWAY
HOME IS WHERE THE HEART IS

The organizing theme for the Cancer/Capricorn polarity is stability and security. Cancer is focused on inner stability and security. It's about how comfortable we feel in our homes and bodies. It's about feeling supported and providing support for others.

The most significant work we can do in Cancer Season is re-parenting ourselves. We've talked about how Cancer energy is typically associated with our early home, roots, and sense of family. We all carry some baggage from our upbringing, and Cancer Season is a perfect time to ask ourselves what we needed and maybe didn't get enough of in our childhood. Even if your childhood experience was relatively good, nothing is perfect. Cancer season teaches us that emotional stability is learning to rely on ourselves to meet our emotional needs and inner sense of security. The fact is, as much as we'd like to believe that other people can be responsible for our emotional state, no one can be everything to or for us. At a certain point, we have to be able to identify our needs and provide that support for ourselves.

Part of that work is leaning into our emotional shifts. Emotional intelligence and introspection aren't often valued in our western capitalistic culture. We're often taught not to cry, show weakness or vulnerability, or be too emotional. But despite our tough exterior "crab shell," we're all somewhat vulnerable inside. Cancer Season is a great time to dive inward and allow ourselves to explore those emotions that we've been taught to conceal. To do this, we need to feel safe. We need a space where we can be relaxed. This is where the focus on our present-day homes comes into play. Our homes provide us with the shielding and protection necessary for this kind of vulnerability.

Finally, we can't talk about Cancer Season without discussing the sense of "birthing" and nurturing something. No, I'm not talking literal babies. (Although, that is one aspect of Cancer energy.) In a broader sense, we can birth businesses or art, for example. The birth process can be uncomfortable for anything we bring into the world. Labor is difficult. But, at its center, Cancer energy embodies a sense of hope where we know "the juice will most certainly be worth the squeeze."

CANCER

Waves-
>Ebbs and flows at the mercy of the moon's pull. (Humans are 70% water.)

Fresh-baked cookies -
>Crispy on the outside. (Gooey on the inside.)

The dank odor of antique stores and attics -
>Scent compounds being the only thing left lingering from loved ones passed. (Olfactory signals straight to our limbic systems. The science behind scent and memory.)

Seeds sprouting, a baby's first steps -
>Confirmation that you're giving them what they need to grow. (Pat yourself on the back. #momlife.)

A hurricane -
>Water isn't always still or linear. (The Coriolis Effect hard at work.)

A crab scuttling sideways -
>So as never to move into the path of another crab. (How considerate.)

A lioness protecting cubs -
>Fighting tooth and claw. (Back up, bitch.)

A motivational poster, a cheerleader -
>Remember that Bette Midler song? (...something about being the wind beneath my wings.)

Salty ocean water -
>Salty tears. (Happy, sad, angry...Name an emotion - any emotion, and we'll shower it in saltwater.)

Familiar layouts of family homes, the symphony of creaks and squeaks, a song we know by heart-
>Blindfold me. Rig the space with Rube Goldberg contraptions a la Home Alone. (I know every inch of this place in my bones. I'll be just fine.)

A weighted blanket -
>The cells in our bodies remembering the simple comfort of being swaddled. (Nothing can get you. You're safe under here.)

Adhesive -
>People embracing. (A child clinging to a parent's leg.)

A home alarm system -
>A security guard. (Safety first.)

It's like Gloria Gaynor said -
>She's a Cancer 7th House cusp, you know? (I will survive.)

75

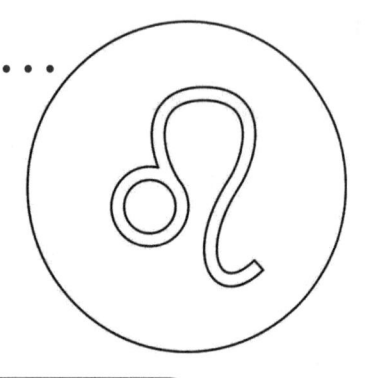

LEO

- **DATES:** JULY 23 - AUGUST 22
- **ELEMENT:** FIRE
- **MODALITY:** FIXED
- **RULING PLANET:** SUN
- **HOUSE:** FIFTH
- **PHRASE:** I CREATE
- **GLYPH:** THE LION
- **TAROT CARDS:** 5 OF WANDS, 6 OF WANDS, 7 OF WANDS, QUEEN OF WANDS, STRENGTH, AND THE SUN

LEO SEASON PLAYLIST

USE THE CAMERA APP ON YOUR PHONE TO ACCESS THIS PLAYLIST.

LEO - A BRIEF INTRODUCTION

The Cardinal Water energy of Cancer Season moved us from spring to summer, and now it's time for Fixed Fire to take center stage, literally. Leo Season is hot. Also, if you've ever met a Leo, you already know they know how to make an entrance and own a spotlight.

We're in the thick of summer. The sun is overhead. Nature is in full bloom, just being an absolute show-off. (Sound familiar?) Ok, but in all seriousness, this is the time of year when we're reminded of nature's generosity, another common Leo trait.

We have central air conditioning nowadays, and capitalism stops for nothing. So, we continue going to work. However, historically speaking, Leo Season would have been too hot for getting much work done outdoors. This would have been a period for entertaining, relaxing, and games. Even now, schools are typically out of session during Leo Season. If we're privileged enough, we go on vacations. We hang out and cool off at the pool. It's a time for leisure and enjoyment. The season reminds us that play is a part of the human experience, even as adults. What's the point of all the work we do in our lives if we don't take some time for fun as well, amiright?

After spending Cancer Season focused on nurturing and supporting ourselves and our loved ones, Leo Season snaps us back into our ego. We're reminded of our need to shine and be seen as individuals. There can be an overwhelming urge for self-expression. There's a desire to radiate our light out into the world. We want to visit with friends, build up our confidence, and engage in creative endeavors. We're also reminded of our sense of personal magnetism in Leo Season. (Well, hello there, summer flings!)

It's also the season for standing firm in our sense of self and convictions. Leo rules the heart in our bodies. The season is a period primed for heart-centered personal discoveries and actions, and being of fixed modality, we know how to dig our heels in and stand strong in what our heart is telling us during this time of year.

Alright, pick out your most head-turning outfit, take some selfies, and strut your stuff like you're the star of your own movie, walking in slow motion to a badass song. (I always think of the hallway scene in the movie Jawbreaker.) Leo Season is here, y'all!

LEO (IRL)

We can't really talk about Leo without talking about its opposite sign, Aquarius. The organizing theme for this astrological polar axis is knowing when it's time for teamwork and when it's time to step out from the crowd and take center stage. The Leo half of the polarity is obviously about knowing when it's time for us to step into the spotlight.

Common stereotypes around the Leo archetype use descriptors like arrogant, attention-seeking, and entitled. As always, stereotypes are rooted in some truth. Leo can be somewhat self-centered from time to time. However, we need to ask ourselves if that's really a problem. Narcissism is one thing, but Leo's energy is hardly Narcissus lost in their reflection. It's about discovering a healthy sense of self-worth, and let's face it, many people and industries benefit from our insecurities. The beauty industry, the diet industry, the fashion industry - all of it is designed to capitalize on our negative self-image. So, there's incentive for us to be conditioned not to love (or even like) ourselves. But there is nothing wrong with a self-appreciation and wanting to be seen. We've just been conditioned to think there is. So, I would argue that the self-centered Leo stereotype is not a problem at all. Leo energy understands the value of self-esteem, and that's not a bad thing.

Leo energy feels very heart-centered. There's an earnest, childlike quality present in the archetype. Above all else, it wants to express. It wants to play. It wants romance, and it wants to create. Where Leo falls in our birth chart is where we are in our joy. It's where we approach life like a child. Under Leo's influence, we legitimately enjoy giving and sharing. Ruled by the Sun (you know, just the life-giver of all things, no big deal), it comes as no surprise that Leo is notoriously generous in spirit. It's joyful, and it wants to share that joy with others.

We also can't really talk about Leo without talking about flirtation. There's no denying Leo energy is flirty af, but it's all in good fun. It's in love with love. Grand displays of affection are its raison d'etre. Ask Leo its preferred love language, and it will just reply, "yes." It loves gifts. It loves acts of service. It loves quality time. It loves physical touch and words of affirmation...and this goes both ways. As much as it loves being the recipient of affection, it likes making grand gestures for someone else even more. So get ready to open your heart this Leo Season!

MEET THE SUN

Leo is ruled by the sun, which has a 365-day orbit. So, once a year, we'll experience a solar return (AKA our Birthday), and what's more appropriate for Leo Season than a day that's all about us?

The sun is a planetary placement that even absolute astro-novices know. Picture it. You're out with friends, and someone approaches you and asks, "Hey baby, what's your sign?" When you reply that you're a Leo (because who gets hit on more than Leo?), you're telling them your sun sign.

The sun is considered one of our luminaries, which is just a fancy way of saying that it's a planet that supplies light. Astrologers refer to the sun as our daytime luminary and the moon as our nighttime luminary.

The sun in our birth charts represents our conscious mind. It's our will and "the fuel we burn." It's the filter through which we experience life, and it's the way we express our individuality. Grant Lewi, an astrologer in the '30s and '40s, described the sun as "the psychological bias which will dominate your actions." He also noted, "You may think, dream, imagine, hope to be a thousand things, according to your moon and your other planets: but the sun is what you are, and to be your best self in terms of your Sun is to cause your energies to work along the path in which they will have maximum help from planetary vibrations."

So, the sun is like our central sense of self, but I find it helpful to describe our sun sign as the tone of our self-talk if you're someone who experiences internal dialogue. I only recently learned that some people don't have this! (I'm obviously someone who does, and I'm just going to go ahead and blame my Leo Moon for that right now.) I'm an Aries Sun. So, my sense of self-talk is through a lens of urgency. Everything feels like it needs to be right now. A Gemini Sun might experience self-dialogue that's a bit busy and all over the place. You get the idea.

In astrology, signs are like adjectives or adverbs. They describe "how" a planet will act. The houses represent the "where," as in what area of life. So if you look to where your sun is located in your birth chart, it will show you the style in which you leave your mark on the world and the areas of life where your individuality shines.

IT'S JUST A PHASE...
LEO SEASON MOONS (IRL)

During Leo Season, we typically experience a Leo New Moon and an Aquarius Full Moon.

LEO NEW MOON

As I mentioned earlier, the Leo/Aquarius polarity deals with understanding the balance between stepping into the spotlight and falling into the crowd and working towards common collective goals. In the Leo New Moon, we feel the need to be seen. It's a period that's well-spent on creative ventures. New moons represent a bit of a pause before the waxing moon period, which, under Leo's influence, is filled with a full social calendar, lots of generosity, and maybe even a little bit of showing off. So, get your ideas together for that new song you want to write or that piece of art you want to make. Dig out all your boldest, head-turning outfits. Book a fun outing with friends and loved ones, and make sure you let them know it's your treat! The idea here is to activate your sense of play! Under Leo's influence, we're being asked to look for joy in both our sense of individuality and the mundane tasks in our day-to-day life.

AQUARIUS FULL MOON

The Aquarius Full Moon reminds us of the Aquarian counter-balance in the Leo/Aquarius polarity. I think we've all been around someone who "sucks all the air out of the room," and it can be a lot. Yes, it's essential for all of us to shine as individuals, but sometimes we need to know when it's appropriate to fall back and work with others towards common goals. This full moon also reminds us of the importance of alone time. A social calendar that's too-full leads us straight into the mouth of burnout, and no one is meant to be "on" all the time. This is the superpower of Aquarius. It's simultaneously focused on the greater good of humanity, but also incredibly solitary at the same time. Under the Aquarius Full Moon, we're invited to pull back and spend time with ourselves. We get a chance to recharge while at the same time shifting our focus away from ourselves and over to supporting others. We all have a cause we feel passionately about, and the waning moon phase following the Aquarius Full Moon is a great time to lean into things we can do to enhance the collective experience.

WELCOME HOME
THE 5TH HOUSE (IRL) - THE HOUSE OF CREATIVE JOY

In a natural chart, Leo is associated with the 5th House, and it's often referred to as the "House of Children and Romantic Affairs," which leaves many people scratching their heads. Most people associate romance with the 7th House and sex with the 8th House. That's not incorrect, but our romantic and sexual preferences are a blend of our 5th, 7th, 8th House placements, as well as our Venus and Mars.

The 7th House is a house about deep partnership. So, yes, technically, marriage is ONE of the things we can see in this house (which we'll discuss a bit more later in Libra's Section). However, astrology is old, and historically speaking (and even sometimes in the modern world), marriage wasn't always about love. It was often transactional and arranged for various reasons. So, who we showed romantic interest in may or may not have been the person we actually married. The 5th House represents our romantic preferences, plain and simple. Those may vary from who we enter committed partnerships with or who we are sexually attracted to. There's also the point of children. Since the 5th House is Leo's House, and Leo represents youthful and playful energy, this is where our relationship to children lives in our birth chart. Having planets here doesn't say whether a person will or won't have children. It just shows our relationship to children. It also speaks to our creative identity. So, in short, the organizing theme for this house is "the things we do and create for joy."

The planets are the "doers" in a chart. So, when we see a chart with many planets in the 5th House, we have someone dedicating quite a bit of their energy to creativity and self-expression, romance, play, and children.

Outside of natal planets in the 5th House, transits to our 5th house and 5th house profection years help us continually evolve and refine how we deal with our sense of creative joy. We experience 5th house profection years at ages 4, 16, 28, 40, 52, 64, 76, 88, and 100. As always, we can look to the ruler of the sign on the 5th House cusp, its placement in the chart, and relevant transits for more specific information around what a specific profection year holds for us. So, take a look at your 5th House. What does it tell you about your creative expression and your relationship to romance and children?

TAROT (IRL)
LEO - STRENGTH

Leo is associated with the Strength card in the Major Arcana. Surprising no one, this card deals with strength and resilience. The twist is that it specifically relates to our sense of perseverance being found in a heart-centered place of vulnerability. It's the idea that there is strength in delicate and unfortified things.

The artwork typically shows a human restraining or petting a lion, but it's not aggressive. The human is approaching the lion from a place of love. The lion is consenting to the restraint. There's no struggle or conflict. It's just two creatures being vulnerable with one another. There's mutual trust.

Sure, "petting the lion" (AKA: doing the scary thing) can be stressful and anxiety-inducing. But, sometimes, releasing the need to "put on a brave face" is where we actually find our bravery. It can be as simple as vocalizing the concern. If we can be honest about what we're feeling in our hearts and approach big situations with love, we can often muster the strength we need to do what we need to do, however difficult.

In the Mundane Magick Tarot Deck, I chose a spiderweb as the image for the Strength card. It looks delicate and fragile to the eye, but pound for pound, it's stronger than steel. This is exactly what the Strength card feels like to me.

It's is a reminder of exactly what our hearts are capable of. Humans are can achieve incredible feats when we put our whole hearts into something. So, when you pull the strength card, just know that the thing likely won't be easy. But also, you have precisely what it takes. Feel your feelings. Be open. Be vulnerable. Be honest. Seek out support if you feel you could use it. But, do the thing. You got this.

THE SUN

The Sun, Leo's ruler, is represented by... The Sun in the Major Arcana.

We can't talk about this card without talking a little bit about the card that precedes it in the Major Arcana - The Moon, which we'll discuss at length in the Pisces Section. The Moon is a card that describes periods in our lives when we cannot see things clearly. We're "in the dark" and feeling our way through a situation that isn't clear to us. You can think of the Moon card as being in a dark room. You may be able to make out shapes, but you can't see everything. When we move into The Sun, it's like someone walks into that room and flips on the lights. Suddenly, we can see everything. It's about clarity, releasing our delusions, and seeing what's really there.

There's a common misconception in the tarot community that The Sun is a "happy" card in the Majors, and look, it can be. But, that isn't always the case. Seeing the truth of a situation doesn't always guarantee that we will like the facts, but we must know them and accept them. Even when the truth hurts us, it's always for the best. Remember, the tarot is happening FOR us, not TO us.

Think about someone who suspects infidelity in their relationship. They're in that "Moon" space trying to confirm or deny their suspicions. Then, the Sun card comes along, and they get confirmation that their partner is betraying their agreed-upon relationship parameters. Sure, that doesn't typically feel great. But, it does free this person up to move on, grieve, heal, and eventually find a new relationship that is better for them, where they can hopefully be happier. Conversely, sometimes the stories we make up in our heads don't accurately reflect what's really happening. We can tell ourselves, "oh, that person doesn't like me," but the Sun can come along and show us that sometimes feelings and thoughts are not reality. So, under the influence of The Sun, be open to seeing what's really there.

83

THE QUEEN OF WANDS - FIXED FIRE

Who is the Queen of Wands? This queen is aligned with Fixed Fire energy. It's a water and fire combo, elementally speaking, which is a combination that shouldn't exist in nature, at least not without a bit of alchemy at play. Queens represent mature, stable, adult energy, typically with internal focus.

The Queen of Wands feels like the "witch" of the deck in many ways, and it almost always features a black cat, symbolic of deep intuition and interest in the occult. Super witchy, right?

The archetype blends feeling and action, and it's all about courage, determination, optimism, and confidence. When this queen shows up for us, we know we're the shit. We're very much in touch with the goals that are intuitively right for us, and we have the fiery ambition to actually do the work. As with most fiery cards, we tend to see results quickly. There's a positive and uplifting quality to the Queen of Wands, but don't get it twisted. This queen will defend its territory. It's not afraid of a worthy fight.

The Queen of Wands has always reminded me of "30s energy," and I'll explain what I mean. When we're in our 20s, there's a lot of magickal stuff happening. We're discovering many new things about ourselves and the world, but we're still finding our footing. Most of us are broke and a little unsure of ourselves. As we enter our 30s, we're typically a little more established. We're wiser. We know what we want, we don't care as much what people think of us, and we don't put up with bullshit. Our 30s are steeped in a sense of self-possession and so is this card.

So, when this queen shows up, just know you are powerful and magickal. You are in tune with what you're being called to in the world, and you have what it takes to go after your goals. So, do no harm, but take no shit.

MEET THE COURT (IRL)
MEET THE QUEEN OF WANDS (IRL)

Use the camera on your phone to scan the QR code and access blogs where we'll discuss real life examples of the Queen of Wands.

THE MINOR ARCANA
5 OF WANDS - SATURN IN LEO

COMPETITION - CONFLICT - CREATIVE STRUGGLES

At first glance, the typical depictions of the 5 of Wands read as a fight. There are multiple people with their rods raised. But, upon closer examination, it's not a fight. It's just a bit of fiery chaos. Who knows what the people in the image are doing? It's anyone's guess. But I like to imagine they're trying to build something together, and everyone is trying to be the boss - talking over one another and refusing to listen. We've all put IKEA furniture together with people who thought they had the best strategy for assembly, right? Super annoying, isn't it? This is very that.

These are the moments in life when we experience competition, conflict, and a bit of creative chaos. What it really comes down to is a battle of wills. The 5's are a contraction that prepares us for expansion later in the suit. If you've ever created anything or chased an ambition, then you already know that nothing worth having is possible without a bit of struggle. This 5 is a reminder to be patient, remember the end goal, and look for common ground. It's just a little lesson in effective planning, teamwork, and communication.

6 OF WANDS - JUPITER IN LEO

VICTORY - TRIUMPH - ACHIEVEMENT

We had a taste of conflict in the 5, and we've fought our way through to the other side. We've persevered, and we're the winner. We get to experience the joy of admiration. Well, sort of...

This card typically shows a victor atop a horse, looking down at an adoring crowd. But, here's the catch. When we're at the top, there's nowhere to go but down. So the key to this card is remembering that all the 6's in the deck deal with themes of cooperation and sharing. It's ok to enjoy triumph and achievement. However, we must remember our humility. There's often a target on our backs when we're on top. It's like Cristal says to Nomi in Showgirls, "There's always someone younger and hungrier coming down the stairs behind you." (Yes, this is my favorite movie. No, I will not be taking questions at this time.) So, enjoy this win, but also know that this isn't going to last forever. Act accordingly.

7 OF WANDS - MARS IN LEO

DEFENSE - PROTECTION - PARANOIA

We've tasted victory in the 6, and now we're absolutely convinced someone is coming to take it away in the 7. Maybe they are. Maybe they aren't. That's the thing about the 7. It's less about whether the threat is real or perceived. It's much more about our sense of hypervigilance.

In the Smith Rider Waite artwork, we see a person atop a hill. They look visibly distressed, tired, and confused. They're wearing mismatched shoes and using their wand to "defend" against the other wands we see surrounding the hill. However, we never see actual people holding the rods. We only see the tops of the wands. There's no confirmation that anything at all is under attack. This could all just be a paranoid delusion, as far as we know.

If the 5 was about attaining our position in the 6, the 7 is about maintaining it. It's the feeling of needing to be one step ahead when what we really need is to work on our sense of inner security...and maybe a nap.

PRACTICAL MAGICK
AFFIRM YOURSELF FOR LEO SEASON

As the interest in modern spirituality grows, we hear more and more about the practice of utilizing affirmations. Now, y'all know I'm not a super woo witch, so this isn't going to be a situation where I make false promises about the magick of speaking or writing phrases to yourself everyday. Some people see results with this, and others don't. As it turns out, there's actually some science behind why that's the case. So, let's talk a bit about the psychology behind affirmations.

THE PSYCHOLOGY OF AFFIRMATIONS

Use your phone's camera to scan the QR code & access this bonus content.

LEO SEASON TAROT + JOURNALING PROMPTS
ASK STRENGTH + THE SUN...

These prompts are perfect for Leo Season tarot or even as journaling prompts.

WHAT AM I MOST AFRAID OF? WHAT MAKES ME FEEL THE MOST VULNERABLE?

HOW CAN I APPROACH MY FEARS AND VULNERABILITIES FROM A HEART-CENTERED PLACE?

WHAT IS SOMETHING THAT IS AN ESSENTIAL TRUTH ABOUT MY SENSE OF INDIVIDUALITY?

HOW CAN I BE MORE HONEST WITH MYSELF?

KITCHEN WITCHIN'
HAPPY BIRTHDAY, BITCH!

Since the sun is Leo's ruler, and our Solar Return represents our birthday, I thought I would include my favorite cake pop recipe. They're super sharable (perfect for social Leo), they're very giftable (we all know Leo is generous af), and you can get as extra as you like in terms of decorating them (because we all know that more is more for Leo). Recipe yields 40 pops. Happy Birthday, Bitch!

CAKE POPS
INSTRUCTIONS

1) Preheat oven to 350 degrees and grease a 9-inch pan.

2) Make the cake first. Mix the flour, baking powder, baking soda, and salt in a bowl. Next, use a mixer to combine the butter and sugar together in a separate bowl until they're well-whipped (1-2 minutes). Add the egg and vanilla extract to the whipped butter and sugar and mix on high until everything is combined. With the mixer still going on low, slowly add the dry ingredients and milk. When everything is mixed, pour the batter into the pan, and bake for 30-36 minutes. Remove the cake, and allow it to cool completely.

3) Make the Frosting. Using a mixer, beat the butter on medium for roughly 2 minutes. Add confectioners' sugar, vanilla, and heavy cream with the mixer on low. Increase to high speed and beat for 3 minutes.

4) Crumble the cooled cake into the frosting bowl. Use a mixer on low to combine the cake and frosting. Ensure there are no large clumps.

INGREDIENTS

Cake:
- 1 and 2/3 cups all-purpose flour, leveled
- 1/2 tsp baking powder
- 1/4 tsp baking soda
- 1/2 tsp salt
- 1/2 cup unsalted butter, softened to room temperature
- 1 cup granulated sugar
- 1 large egg
- 2 tsp pure vanilla extract
- 1 cup whole milk or buttermilk

Frosting:
- 7 tbsp unsalted butter, softened to room temperature
- 1 and 3/4 cups confectioners' sugar
- 2-3 tbsp heavy cream or milk
- 1 tsp pure vanilla extract

Coating:
- 40 oz candy melts or coating
- sprinkles
- cake pop or lollipop sticks

5) Measure 1 tbsp of the cake and frosting mixture and roll into a ball. Place the balls on a lined baking sheet. These can be refrigerated for 2 hours or frozen for 1 hour. After they're chilled, you can re-roll the balls to make sure they're smooth. It's best to do this in increments of 2-3 and then place them back into the fridge/freezer as you're done working with them.

6) Prep a cake pop holder to get ready for dipping. If you don't have a fancy one, you can use a styrofoam block or poke holes in a box. You just need to have something to hold the cake pops upright while they set.

6) Melt the candy melts in a cup for dipping. A 2-cup liquid measuring cup works well. You can use a double boiler, but the microwave works too.

7) Remove the cake pops from the fridge/freezer. Dip a cake pop stick 1/2 inch into the coating and then insert it into the center of a cake ball. Only push it roughly halfway inside. Then, dip the cake ball into the coating until it's completely covered. Allow excess coating to drain off. Decorate with sprinkles, and place upright in your cake pop holder. The coating sets in an hour and pops can be stored in the fridge for up to a week.

MORE IS MORE
ELEVATE YOUR MOOD WITH MAXIMALISM FOR LEO SEASON

There's a growing trend in decor and personal style that I'm sure we've all seen somewhere or another on the internet - maximalism.

What is maximalism? It's the art of layering patterns and highly saturated colors and accessories. It creates a sense of boldness and texture in outfits and living spaces, and frankly, nothing screams Leo more loudly than maximalism done well. So, this is absolutely a great season to experiment with it, even in small doses!

Psychological studies have found that what we wear and how we decorate can influence our thinking. Mismatched patterns elicit a feeling of novelty and surprise. Statement colors and accessories make us feel emboldened. Playful patterns make us feel youthful. You get the idea. So, allow yourself the chance to step outside of your comfort zone and try something new for Leo Season. Let maximalism lift your mood!

LEO SEASON WORDS: THE TAKEAWAY
LOVING YOURSELF IS A REVOLUTIONARY ACT

At the beginning of this section, I spoke a bit about how we often perceive Leo energy as arrogant and self-centered when it's really a desire to be witnessed. So, we can't talk about embodying healthy Leo energy without talking about why so many of us struggle with the idea of being seen and putting ourselves out in the world. We also have to discuss capitalism's role in the struggle and its relation to the Leo/Aquarius polarity.

Now, we might think that our self-awareness is a gift. Having insight into how others view us seems like it would be helpful, and in some ways, it is. The Aquarius half of the polarity highly values the needs of the group over the needs of the individual, and sometimes this is necessary. However, what tends to happen is that self-awareness, and specifically self-consciousness, is more of a gift to the people around us. It forces us to calibrate our behavior based on feedback from others. This isn't something that always helps us live more in tune with our own sense of individuality, which the Leo half of the polarity values. It puts a damper on the unique expression of our creativity and talents for others' comfort, and it doesn't always make relationships any easier to navigate.

We also have to consider that a core value of capitalism is competition. We all live in capitalism, whether we like it or not. In a competitive environment, which includes most spaces in a capitalistic culture, we can be incentivized to cut one another down. The entire system is built upon stepping on others as we climb to "the top." So, when someone is shining brightly, society can be tempted to "take them down a peg." Capitalism relies on us keeping one another small. We often feel a sense of trepidation around sharing ourselves and our creations with the world because we inherently know that the world can be cruel and judgmental. So, we become hyper-aware of anything we do that could potentially elicit negative feedback from others, but Leo Season isn't the time for that.

With any astrological polarity, the balance is in the middle. If we all allowed one another the unique expression of individuality without judgment, we would become stronger and more united as a collective. The first step starts with us. Leo Season is a reminder that loving ourselves is a revolutionary act. It flies in the face of oppressive systems. If we are committed to loving ourselves, we are more open to the idea of loving others. So give yourself a little love this Leo Season.

LEO

The warmth of stage lighting -
      Please, photos from my good side only... (Who am I kidding? They're both great. Obviously.)
Oxytocin -
      A rain-soaked Mr. Darcy proposing to Elizabeth. Patrick serenading Kat on the soccer field. Lloyd holding up a boombox outside of Diane's window. "No one puts Baby in a corner," and of course, an elaborate choreographed dance number. (The grand gesture is truly a lost art.)
A phone dings and chimes with social media notifications.
      You like me. You really like me. (Don't forget to like and subscribe.)
Buttercream frosting -
      Feining embarrassment as the waitstaff brings over a cake and the entire room sings "Happy Birthday." (They're all looking at you...and isn't it great?)
Julie Andrews as Mary Poppins-
      "In every job that must be done, there is an element of fun. You find the fun and...snap! The job's a game!" (A spoonful of sugar does indeed help the medicine go down...)
Good hair day -
      It used to be thought that lion's manes were an evolutionary advantage that protected their necks during scuffles. As it turns out, it's the lion equivalent of a peacock's tail, mane-ly used to attract a mate. (See what I did there?)
A smock covered in paint -
      Create like no one's watching (even though everyone is)
A hand moves swiftly to pick up the check -
      "I got it. No, seriously, it's my treat." (My paternal grandmother's voice, "You don't have to be rich to be generous.")
A slow-motion walk, wind in the hair -
      Wasn't it Coco Chanel who said, "Dress like you're going to meet your worst enemy today?" (The best revenge truly is living well. She was a Leo, you know? Of course, she was.)
Beauty industry ads -
      "Eliminate your flaws! Erase all evidence that you're a real person!" (But you know better, don't you? You're perfect the way you are.)

VIRGO

- DATES: AUGUST 23 - SEPTEMBER 22
- ELEMENT: EARTH
- MODALITY: MUTABLE
- RULING PLANET: MERCURY
- HOUSE: SIXTH
- PHRASE: I ANALYZE
- GLYPH: THE VIRGIN/THE MAIDEN
- TAROT CARDS: 8 OF PENTACLES, 9 OF PENTACLES, 10 OF PENTACLES, KNIGHT OF PENTACLES, AND THE HERMIT

VIRGO SEASON PLAYLIST

USE THE CAMERA APP ON YOUR PHONE TO ACCESS THIS PLAYLIST.

VIRGO - A BRIEF INTRODUCTION

It's late summer. Things are starting to cool off. A wave of Mutable Earth energy washes over us, preparing us for the shift from summer to fall. We feel pulled back to our work and sense of duty after spending much of Leo Season focused on creativity and play. The signs of preparatory Virgo energy are all around us. We're shopping for school supplies and getting ready for the new school year. It's also the traditional time of year for harvesting crops to sustain us throughout the coming fall and winter months. We start thinking about digging out our jackets and sweaters for cooler weather. Planning is in the air!

Because Virgo leans into hard work, there can be some cross-over in traits with fellow earth sign, Capricorn. The two do share a mutual love for completing tasks, but there is a critical difference, and it's in their core motivation and how they like to be perceived. Capricorn likes to be seen as competent, while Virgo prefers to be seen as useful. It's all about being of service. This distinction is one of the keys to understanding Virgo energy. Virgo is here to help, and one of its ultimate goals is improvement. There's a strong desire to create organization in the areas of our lives that need it, and Virgo shines when it can build effective systems that make our lives easier.

The stereotypes of Virgo being overly-critical and hyper-focused on details aren't entirely unwarranted. However, we must take a moment to understand why this is the case. It has everything to do with the archetype "stamp" on the time of year. As I mentioned, historically, Virgo Season would be the season when humans harvested what was planted in the spring. The harvest, itself, would be a lot of work, but Virgo doesn't mind. Staying busy is good for the Mercurial sign. After the harvest, it's decision-making time. Survival in the colder months would be heavily dependent on Virgo Season's decisions. Those decisions would include determining what crops were good/bad, how much food should be stored to last the winter, what should be held to plant in the following spring, and what should be reserved to feed livestock. A miscalculation could mean the literal difference between life or death.

In this way, Virgo is kind of like the quality control or quality assurance department of the zodiac. They need to be able to make the tough calls regarding what passes or fails against a set of criteria. So, dust off those planners. It's Virgo Season!

VIRGO (IRL)

As always, we have to begin the discussion about Virgo by discussing the astrological polarity it belongs to. Virgo's polar sign is Pisces. The organizing theme for the Virgo/Pisces axis is devotion and healing. Where watery Pisces teaches us how to lean into spiritual/emotional devotion and intuitive healing, earthly Virgo is the concept's physical manifestation. It's about how we create structure and use our bodies for acts of service in the earthly realm. It's also how we care for our bodies.

All earth signs are focused on the physical plane somehow or another. They're tied to our homes, sensual experiences (as in, the things we take in with our five senses), material wealth, and bodies, and Virgo is VERY in tune with the body. When we think about the fact that Virgo is so in tune with details, so skilled at identifying abnormalities, and so focused on being of service, it makes sense that they have a natural talent for diagnosis and healing. There's a sense of diagnostic intuition and instinctual knowledge of both pharmaceutical and natural medicine. There's a big focus on health and the human body present in Virgo energy.

It's also no secret that Mercury-ruled signs are a bit nervous by design. When we blend this with interest in health the highly-strung Mercurial qualities, we can see a touch of germophobia or a general preoccupation with cleanliness, another common Virgo stereotype. The symbol for Virgo is the Virgin, which is universally tied to the idea of purity. Please note that this is not to say that virgins are pure and non-virgins are not. I'm strictly speaking about the symbolism of the word. The word's literal definition is "not yet touched, used, or exploited," and this extends beyond human sexuality. For example, undyed natural hair is often called "virgin hair" within the cosmetology industry, and untouched forests are sometimes referred to as "virgin forests."

This leads us to the central essence of Virgo energy, the idea of ease and beauty in untouched things. There's an intuitive sense of order in the physical plane, and Virgo's imperative is to be of service to it. When the sun makes its trip through Virgo each year, we're all illuminated with Virgo energy. It's a great time of year for planning, cleaning, organizing, being of service, and taking care of our bodies.

MEET MERCURY (AGAIN)

Mercury has dual rulership over Gemini (which we've already discussed) and Virgo. Since we've already talked about the planet itself and how it relates to Gemini, I want to take a minute to focus on the differences between how Mercury shows up differently in the Gemini and Virgo archetypes.

The main difference between the two signs is their elemental influence. Gemini is the airy expression of the planet, and Virgo is the earthly expression. The Gemini performance of Mercurial energy is curious and communicative. Virgo's is earthy, structured, and tangible. While they both have busy minds, Gemini has a dynamic and talkative nature, while Virgo has an active body.

Mercury energy shines through Virgo in how we plan and troubleshoot issues here on the physical plane. While Gemini prefers to go with the flow, Virgo prefers preparation. (Virgo seriously tends to hate surprises.) Gemini can sometimes focus more on discussion and conceptual understanding than action. Virgo likes to get its hands in the dirt and do the work.

Both Gemini and Virgo are Mercurial in the sense that they have a natural tendency toward logic over emotion. This isn't to say that they don't have or value emotions. Of course, they do. What we're talking about here is kind of like a preferred filter or order of operations. (An elementary school math reference - how Virgo is that?) Just as some of the more intuitive signs in the zodiac tend to view logic through a lens of emotion and instinct, Mercurial signs like Gemini and Virgo tend to do the opposite. They have a natural preference to analyze and intellectualize their feelings and intuition.

The Virgo expression of Mercury feels very rooted in good, old-fashioned, practical common sense. Its skill set shines where efficiency and optimization are required. Virgo has a powerful sense of functional understanding. It doesn't want to build systems simply for the sake of doing it. Everything needs to have a purpose and provide some measure of improvement for the end-user. Otherwise, what's the point?

IT'S JUST A PHASE...
VIRGO SEASON MOONS (IRL)

During Virgo Season, we typically experience a Virgo New Moon and a Pisces Full Moon.

VIRGO NEW MOON

Virgo new moons are a great time to examine our mind/body connection as well as our habits and routines. Are there things you might like to approach with a better sense of organization? Maybe there are spaces in your home or workspace that could use a little overhaul? (I'm looking at you, Tupperware cabinet.) Maybe you want to experiment with a new planner layout? Or perhaps there are some things you'd like to do for your health and body? (No, this isn't about toxic diet culture. That isn't the essence of Virgo.) For instance, maybe you sense that you're not getting enough sleep, and you'd like to create some better sleep hygiene habits. Another good example would be drinking more water (especially if you're like me, and you'd be delighted to survive on black coffee all day). The idea is that the Virgo new moon is a pause to think about reinventing your habits. It's a time to make plans for improvements.

PISCES FULL MOON

As you've probably gathered, Virgo is deeply rooted in devotion to the practical, tangible, and analytical world around us. The Pisces full moon in the middle of Virgo Season comes as a welcome reminder that a sense of preparation and being grounded in the reality of the physical plane is cool and all. Still, the universe is mysterious and unknowable in many ways. Time isn't linear. Dreams are magickal, and much of our existence is something that can't be tangibly perceived. So, while it can be tempting to plan and prepare for every possible thing, it's simply not feasible. This full moon is a reminder to leave room for mystery and allow our sense of intuition to take the wheel from time to time, even if it isn't the "practical" thing to do. During Pisces full moons, pay special attention to your dreams, forget your schedule, dive into your spiritual practice (tarot, astrology, crystals...however it looks for you). Be mindful of the fact that we don't and can't know everything, and believing in something we can't necessarily "see" or "prove" is part of the human experience.

WELCOME HOME
THE 6TH HOUSE (IRL) - THE HOUSE OF DAILY RHYTHM + OUR BODIES

Virgo is associated with the 6th House in a natural chart, and it's often referred to as the "House of Daily Work as a Form of Service and The Physical Body." People are often confused about how this is different from the 10th House, where our careers ordinarily live in the birth chart. The significant distinction is that the 6th House tends to tell us about the daily rhythm we prefer and how that ties to our physical health. The 10th House is typically connected to our ambitions and public reputation, which our career tends to fall into.

Now, to make this distinction a bit more clear, we have to think about early humans. If we were all living in a group, as cavepeople did, there would be a distinct division of labor. One of us might be a forager. Another might be responsible for hunting. These wouldn't exactly be our "passion projects," but they would be daily work that was crucial to our survival and primarily determined the rhythm of our day. The fact that failure in these areas could mean death implies that there is a part of the human experience and our physical health and wellness that is tied to working daily for a purpose, contributing, and being of service to the larger group.

The 6th House is a house about our preferred daily flow. If someone has Pisces on the 6th House cusp, they may procrastinate and struggle with rigid schedules. Aries on the 6th House cusp may feel a constant sense of urgency to complete everything they need to accomplish throughout the day. The 6th House tells us a lot about what work environments would be good for us, and as always, the planets are the "doers" in a chart. So, when we see a chart with many planets in the 6th House, we have someone dedicating quite a bit of their energy to being of service, being a "worker bee," and the physical body. Various planets in the 6th House can also be eerily accurate predictors for potential health issues a person may face.

Outside of natal planets in the 6th House, transits to our 6th House and 6th House profection years help us continually evolve and refine how we show up in work, service, and our bodies. We experience 6th House profection years at ages 5, 17, 29, 41, 53, 65, 77, 89, and 101. As always, we can look to the ruler of the sign on the 6th House cusp, its placement in the chart, and relevant transits for more specific information around what a specific profection year holds for us.

TAROT (IRL)
VIRGO - THE HERMIT

Virgo is associated with The Hermit in the Major Arcana. Hermit artwork traditionally shows a person (usually an older person), alone, climbing a mountain with only the light of their lantern guiding them. The symbolism implies that wisdom is found when we can slow our pace, find quiet seclusion, and put one foot in front of the other.

I always think of caterpillars becoming butterflies when I think of Hermit energy. It suggests that parts of maturing and transformation can only be done in solitude. There's also a common misconception that Hermit energy is about being lazy or lounging around alone. But this is Virgo's card, and Virgo is nothing if not a hard worker. While Hermit energy may not be "busy," at least in the sense that we traditionally think of business, it's doing hard work. The pace is slower and more deliberate, but a significant transformation is happening in the Hermit.

Think about what happens when a caterpillar is shifting into a butterfly. First, it builds itself a cocoon, creating isolation. Then, a slow and steady process begins. Their bodies instinctively know to release an enzyme that dissolves them entirely. Yes, this is actually how it happens. They become a sort of nutrient-rich soup from which a butterfly begins to form. This process reminds us that to be privy to instinctual wisdom and able to mature and transform, we sometimes have to slow down, isolate, and do the work.

Now, we can't forget the most essential part. After the caterpillar is transformed into a butterfly, it leaves the cocoon and returns to its community. The same is true for us. Hermit spaces are not forever. We always return to society to share what we've learned in our growth.

THE KNIGHT OF PENTACLES - MUTABLE EARTH

Who is the Knight of Pentacles? This knight is aligned with Mutable Earth energy. It blends airy intellect with earthy practicality and work ethic.

Knights represent qualities of movement through the world, and this knight is all about reliability and commitment to the tasks at hand. Each action is deliberate and goal-oriented but rarely rushed. Most of the other knights in the deck look like they're on a quest or adventure, especially in some of the more traditional tarot artwork. But, the Knight of Pentacles always feels more like it prefers to be at home, doing focused work on its projects.

When we're in a Knight of Pentacles space, we're methodically completing small daily tasks to reach our long-term goals. This knight understands that the chances of big windfalls are few and far between. The odds of winning the lottery are slim to none, and the best way to build something secure for ourselves is to play the long game.

So, when you cross paths with the Knight of Pentacles, it's an indication to slow your pace and focus on the small doses of work that need to be done consistently to reap the larger results at some point in the future. This can be career-related, obviously. However, it can also be about making the change to start a regular fitness practice or even to the smaller steps we need to take in building a sense of security and stability in our relationships.

This knight inherently understands that nothing worth having usually comes quickly or easily and that slow and steady wins the race. So, embrace your sense of structure and dedication, and keep on keeping on.

MEET THE COURT (IRL)
MEET THE KNIGHT OF PENTACLES

Use the camera on your phone to scan the QR code and access blogs where we'll discuss real life examples of the Knight of Pentacles.

THE MINOR ARCANA
8 OF PENTACLES - SUN IN VIRGO

APPRENTICESHIP - COMMITMENT - PRACTICE

In the 8 of Pentacles, we often see a person sitting at a workbench. They're entirely focused on their work, etching coin after coin. The image also frequently shows a town far in the distance, which indicates that this person is in isolation, working on their craft. This card is the essence of "practice makes perfect" or "sucking at something's the first step to being sort of good at something." When we're in 8 of Pentacles space, we have a dream or a goal but not yet the requisite skills to achieve it. In this 8, we learn to put the work in. My great-grandfather used to tell me that "you can do anything you put your mind to." While he wasn't entirely incorrect, there was a missing piece. Our minds and our wills are important, but we also have to be willing to put in the sweat equity. Many modern spiritual circles are positively obsessed with the idea of manifestation. Well, this is manifestation in the purest sense of the word. Lighting a carved colored candle alone won't get you your dream job. It can help you focus your intentions, but you have to attain the required skills and apply for it. I know it may not be glamorous, but this is what real-life manifestation work looks like.

9 OF PENTACLES - VENUS IN VIRGO

SUCCESS - REWARDED EFFORTS - ABUNDANCE

After putting in all that work in the 8 of Pentacles, we find ourselves comfortable in our success in the 9. Of course, being Venus in Virgo energy, the first thing that comes to mind is material wealth. While that's certainly a thing in the 9 of Pentacles, it's also bigger than that. It's a moment of reflection when we can look back over all of the work and dedication we've poured into something, and somehow, it all seems worth it.

The card traditionally features imagery of a person looking positively luxurious. They appear confident and secure, usually dressed in expensive clothing, in front of vines blooming with fruit, flowers, and pentacles.

The 9 of Pentacles typically represents periods when we're self-sufficient and thriving. So, enjoy it!

10 OF PENTACLES - MERCURY IN VIRGO

LEGACY - TRADITION - INHERITANCE

The energy of the 9 of Pentacles expands into the 10. In the 10, we've built something so stable and abundant. It has the capacity to outlive us. The traditional artwork shows elders surrounded by children, grandchildren, and pets. The elders appear to be taking in and enjoying everything they've worked so diligently to build. The elders are dressed in gowns decorated in crescent moons and fruit, representing the merger between our spiritual nature and material abundance.

The 10 of Pentacles shows us the moments when we've made choices that benefit us not only in the present, as we experience in the 9, but far into the future. We've created something so solid and sustainable that it will benefit our loved ones for generations to come. There's also a super appreciative and humbling quality to this card. This isn't unearned wealth. It's not giving Kardashian energy. The work required to reach this point is true boot-strapping. So, there's an awareness of where we've come from.

PRACTICAL MAGICK
VIRGO SEASON

As you've probably gathered by now, if we aren't using Virgo Season to get focused and organized, we've misunderstood the assignment in a big way. Virgo is also notoriously anxious. So, for Virgo Season, bullet journaling is a great way to create new habits and structure in our lives. As an added bonus, the creative component of bullet journaling offers some much needed stress relief. If you can dream it, there's a bullet journal layout specifically for it.

GET IT TOGETHER, BITCH.

Use your phone's camera to scan the QR code & access this bonus content.

VIRGO SEASON TAROT + JOURNALING PROMPTS
ASK THE HERMIT...

These prompts are perfect for Virgo Season tarot or even as journaling prompts.

WHAT AREAS OF MY LIFE COULD BENEFIT FROM MORE GROUNDED STRUCTURE?

HOW CAN I BEST BE OF SERVICE IN THE WORLD?

WHAT IS THE PRESENT SOLO TRANSFORMATIONAL WORK THAT ONLY I CAN DO?

WHAT WISDOM DO I HAVE TO SHARE WITH THE WORLD?

WHAT DATA WOULD BE BENEFICIAL FOR ME RIGHT NOW?

KITCHEN WITCHIN'
GET WELL SOON

Virgo is health-conscious and always willing to lend a helping hand. Virgo moon placements in a birth chart are often referred to as "medicine-chest moons." They are notably skilled in taking care of people who have fallen under the weather. So, the recipe that came to mind for Virgo was immediately this soup. It's a staple in our household when we're under the weather (and when we're not). It's seriously delicious. Recipe yields 6 servings.

CREAMY HERB, CHICKEN, AND MUSHROOM SOUP

INSTRUCTIONS

1) Heat olive oil in a large pot over medium heat. Dry and season the diced chicken thighs and season with salt and pepper. Add the chicken and cook for 5 minutes until it's cooked through. Set aside.

2) Melt the butter over medium heat and add the garlic, mushrooms, onion, carrots, and celery. Cook until tender for 3-4 minutes. Stir in the thyme, and cook until fragrant, about 1 minute.

3) Whisk in flour until it's lightly browned. Then slowly whisk in the chicken stock. Finally, add the bay leaf and cooked chicken from step 1 back into the pot.

INGREDIENTS
- 1 tbsp olive oil
- 8 oz boneless, skinless chicken thighs, cut into bite-sized pieces
- salt and Pepper
- 2 tbsp Butter
- 3 cloves of garlic, peeled and minced
- 8 oz cremini mushrooms, sliced
- 1 onion, diced
- 3 carrots, peeled and diced
- 2 stalks celery, diced
- 1/2 tsp dried thyme
- 1/4 cup all-purpose flour
- 4 cups chicken stock
- 1 bay leaf
- 1/2 cup heavy cream (maybe more, if you like your soup on the creamier side)
- 2 tbsp chopped Italian parsley
- 1 sprig fresh rosemary

4) Stir in half and half, and season with salt and pepper to taste. If the soup is too thick, you can add additional chicken stock or half and half until the desired consistency is reached.

5) Garnish with rosemary sprig and serve immediately. (I like to serve it with a warm baguette.)

VIRGO SEASON WORDS: THE TAKEAWAY
THERE IS ONLY ONE WAY TO EAT AN ELEPHANT

If you're into anything remotely witchy, you can't log onto social media without being inundated with posts talking about manifestation and abundance work, and Virgo is the OG manifestor. I know this is energy we might be tempted to associate with the Capricorn archetype at first glance, but Virgo energy is manifestation work in it's purest form.

Here's the thing. So many people think that manifestation work is largely about pageantry. But, going after the things we want is so much more than simply doing a spell. This isn't to say that ritual isn't important. It is. Humans inherently understand the importance of ritual. Hell, it's why we make a wish and blow out the candles on our birthday cakes. But, we have to understand that ritual is also largely symbolic. It's a way of marking time or focusing our intentions. Ritual without action in our day to day lives is essentially useless.

True manifestation work is physical devotion to a goal, and that's the very essence of Virgo. Sure, tackling big things can be intimidating. This is where the genius of Virgo comes in. It's like when Desmond Tutu said, "There is only one way to eat an elephant: one bite at a time." Virgo understands that anything worth having comes with work, patience, and dedication.

Once we have a defined goal, the real life magick is in the planning and execution. Sure, we can do rituals to focus ourselves and remind ourselves why we're doing the thing. But, the real progress comes from creating the structures in our daily lives that deliver the future results we want. It's not about instant gratification. It's about being so committed to what we're trying to manifest that we're ok with the fact that the results won't be immediate.

Grit is defined as "passion and perseverance for long-term and meaningful goals," and psychologists have found that grit, as a personality trait, is the single biggest predictor of success. Some researchers believe grit is innate, while others suggest that this is mindset that can be developed. For those who are of the latter school of thought, it could certainly be argued that one of the primary goals of Virgo energy is to help us develop grit.

So, you want the thing, what are you gonna do about it?

VIRGO

Spreadsheets and databases -
    Rules, facts, and figures. (Let's just look at the data before we make any big decisions, ok?)
A quality control worker -
    Meets Specifications or Does not Meet Specifications. Yes or No. Good or Bad. Pass or Fail. In or Out. There is no in-between. (It's a tough job, but someone's gotta do it.)
Preparatory Proverbs -
    "Measure twice, cut once." "An ounce of prevention is worth a pound of cure." (Concise, yet full of wisdom).
Setting alarms -
    And waking up five minutes before they go off. (You know what they say, "the early bird gets the worm.")
Web MD bookmarked on a browser -
    A cabinet full of herbal teas. (It'll cure what ails ya.)
A feed full of cleaning videos -
    Who knew bleaching grout could be so supremely satisfying? (Gotta have something to watch when I'm too nervous to sleep.)
The uncontrollable urge to straighten something -
    It's just like Radiohead said on Kid A. (Everything in its Right Place.)
Chalky Tums -
    The electric pink of Pepto Bismol. (A nervous mind expressed as a nervous tummy.)
A hand-written letter -
    Perfect penmanship. (Because when do we ever have a chance to show that off these days?)
Neatly appointed stacks of books-
    Color-coded and in alphabetical order. (I'm a Dewey decimal system unto myself.)
The tightness of freshly washed skin -
    The kind of minimal beauty that doesn't need accessorizing.
Darts sticking out of a bullseye -
    The human embodiment of both accuracy and precision.
The safety of a plan, perfectly executed -
    It's only because somewhere inside, you understand. (The world is a wild place, and try as we may, planning does not always guarantee security.)

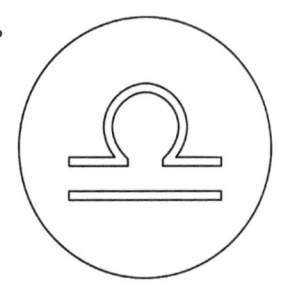

LIBRA

- **DATES:** SEPTEMBER 23 - OCTOBER 22
- **ELEMENT:** AIR
- **MODALITY:** CARDINAL
- **RULING PLANET:** VENUS
- **HOUSE:** SEVENTH
- **PHRASE:** I BALANCE
- **GLYPH:** THE SCALES
- **TAROT CARDS:** ACE OF SWORDS, 2 OF SWORDS, 3 OF SWORDS, 4 OF SWORDS, PAGE OF SWORDS, KING OF SWORDS, AND JUSTICE

LIBRA SEASON PLAYLIST

USE THE CAMERA APP ON YOUR PHONE TO ACCESS THIS PLAYLIST.

LIBRA - A BRIEF INTRODUCTION

After the Mutable Earth energy of Virgo Season, the sun moves into the Cardinal Air of Libra Season. The Autumn Equinox marks the start of the second half of the year. The first half of the year, kicked off by polar sign, Aries, is the solar half of the year. The second half of the year is darker and colder. Fall is here, baby!

Aries Season kicked off the astrological new year six months earlier, which began a cycle closely linked with individual expression. The days got longer and longer from spring into the summer. Now, as we reach Aries' polar sign, Libra, and the days get shorter and shorter, we've pulled away from a focus on the self and personal pursuits in favor of seeking comfort with others. It's time to shift the focus from "me" to "we."

Collaboration is an essential quality for this time of year. In Virgo Season, crops are harvested, and we would begin the planning process for resource management to last us through the colder months. Following the Virgo Season groundwork, Libra Season is the period where we carry out the plans. It's the last opportunity to tie up any loose ends before the weather starts to get notably colder in Scorpio Season. This requires an awareness of others in the community and cooperation among those community members to make sure everything is ready for the months ahead. It also requires us to look at all the potential outcomes for managing finite resources to determine the best and most balanced course of action, typically through a democratic process or majority rule. This is all the essence of Libra.

This is the season for balance, most notably the balance between ourselves and others. Libra Season brings a sense of sociability and focuses on fairness and diplomacy. As the cooler weather approaches, we lean into Libra's natural sense of aesthetic by layering our fall wardrobe and creating cozy, stylish spaces to hang out in the colder weather. The leaves are beginning to change color, a proper Venusian display. Lastly - who could forget the official start of pumpkin spice lattes and gorgeous latte art season? (Is there anything more Libra?)

Grab your favorite apple or pumpkin treat, and get comfortable. It's Libra Season!

LIBRA (IRL)

Libra values harmony and relationships, and the one-word descriptor that comes to mind is "charm." Libra is undeniably charming. It could sell a snow cone to a penguin. The first four people I seriously dated were all Libras, and man oh man... they've got charisma.

Libra values consensus and cooperation over conflict, which can be a gift and a struggle. Unlike its polar sign, notorious hot-head, Aries, Libra thinks (and overthinks) about the long-term consequences of quarreling with others. On the one hand, having such a keen awareness of cause and effect gives Libra a sense of perspective and enables it to avoid damaging relationships over the small stuff. On the flip side, as much as Libra may dislike it, conflict is an unavoidable part of life. Avoidance of confrontation does not absolve us of conflict. It just changes the way it looks. Rather than being outwardly aggressive, we see a tendency toward passive aggression.

The ideas of justice and fairness are also central to Libra. The Libra archetype represents legal systems, specifically court systems. So it makes sense when we consider Libra's ability to evaluate both sides of an argument and make balanced judgments. This is the case in day-to-day life as well. It's where the classic Libra stereotype of being more than a little indecisive comes from.

A straightforward example can show so many Libra traits in action. Ask Libra what it wants to do for dinner. You will undoubtedly be met with long pensive silence or a "you choose." With so many options to consider, there's an imperative to make "the right decision" (even in instances when there isn't necessarily "a right decision" to be made). It's also because Libra is trying to consider what YOU might like for dinner, which shows the other major stereotype for considering others' needs alongside (and sometimes even before) its own. This latter tendency is a beneficial skill in so many ways, but in other ways, it can lend itself to struggles with chronic people-pleasing behavior.

Lastly, we can't talk about Libra (IRL) without mentioning the impeccable sense of aesthetic the sign is so well-known for. Libra is stylish af, and while it may take a little time finalizing a look or home decor or a web design, it will be undeniably RIGHT when it's done.

MEET VENUS (AGAIN)

We've already discussed Venus related to Taurus, but Venus has dual rulership over Libra. While the Taurus expression of Venus is heavily grounded in earthy themes such as the material world and sensual experiences, the Libra expression focuses on the airy Venusian concepts of relationships and a refined sense of intellect.

We've established that Venus is the planet of love, beauty, and refinement, but that can be expressed in more ways than exclusively the material stuff. Venus cares about the beauty in human connection, relationships, merging, and consideration for others and ideas. This is where Libra's imperative lies.

I spoke in the Taurus section about how our natal Venus sign can tell us about what we find valuable and how we experience pleasure. Now, the Libra part of our Venus sign is responsible for describing how we prefer to socialize, what we're attracted to, who is attracted to us, who and how we are in relationships, and how we express our desires. Venus loves love, and Libra is the poster child.

Venus shining through Libra also shows us the ability to hold space for multiple possibilities simultaneously. It's a sort of gentle and open consideration for all sides of a thing - a decision, a court case, a fight, etc. Where many zodiac signs rely on a solid sense of impulse and judgment (as is their imperative), Libra brings open-mindedness and empathy to the evaluation and decision-making processes.

This Venusian filter over Libra's ability to hear all the evidence and deliberate doesn't absolve it of a strong sense of justice. Libra and Aries are united in that one of the most egregious offenses in their eyes is something that "just isn't fair." While Aries roots for the underdog from a place of spite and enjoying a challenge, Libra does so from a place of deep sensitivity. It's about making sure "the little guy's" voice is heard.

We traditionally think of airy energy as being more head than heart. Libra's expression of Venus is the exception to this stereotype, blending head and heart in a way that shows us what real balance looks like.

IT'S JUST A PHASE...
LIBRA SEASON MOONS (IRL)

During Libra Season, we typically experience a Libra New Moon and an Aries Full Moon.

LIBRA NEW MOON

Libra New Moons are a time for looking at our relationships through a gentle yet critical lens. If there are things that we think we could be doing better or we have needs that aren't being met, now is the time to start planning that work. If we're in a romantic relationship, this is a great time to check in with our partner(s) and have some candid discussion. If we're open to it, couples counseling sessions are beneficial during this time. Libra is a natural mediator, and sessions with Libra New Moon energy behind them can be highly productive. Even outside of romantic relationships, the Libra New Moon is a time for us to shift our focus to improved connection with others across the board. This can also be friendships and family. Despite our best intentions, we all have "that friend" that we haven't been able to connect with for a long time. (Hey, life gets busy!) The Libra New Moon is a great time to reach out and say, "Long time, no see! Let's grab coffee!"

ARIES FULL MOON

The Aries Full Moon comes to pull us back into our sense of individuality. This full moon asks us to remember to balance the needs of others with our personal desires. This full moon also reminds us that while the measured and carefully thought-out energy of Libra Season is great, all things are best in moderation. Sometimes we need to be impulsive and trust our gut without questioning it to death. The go-getter within us gets a little jolt during the Aries Full Moon, as does our physical drive. It's a great time to release pent-up energy in the body through physical activity or work on a project tied to an important personal goal. This is also a time to be blunt. While Libra energy values refined and diplomatic conversation, the Aries Full Moon reminds us that sometimes we need to simply say what we mean. Some messages aren't meant to be delivered gently. It's an excellent time for honesty and creating firm boundaries. The takeaway from this full moon is that we can't be available for others if we aren't caring for ourselves.

WELCOME HOME
THE 7TH HOUSE (IRL) - THE HOUSE OF PARTNERSHIP

Libra is associated with the 7th House. It's often called the "House of Partnerships." The main areas of focus for Libra Season and the 7th House are relationships, deep one-to-one partnerships, and legal matters.

The sign that sits on the cusp of the 7th House in our natal chart is what we refer to as our descendant. It's the sign that was setting in the sky at the time of our birth.

If the sign on our 1st House cusp is how we meet the world, then the sign on our 7th House cusp tells us how we partner out in the world. This includes deep romantic commitments (such as marriage), close friendships, contracts, negotiations, and business collaborations. It describes the role(s) we play in deep partnership, who we attract, and our relationships' general vibe. It's also the house that shows things like divorces and lawsuits. It's important to note that parts of what we're romantically and sexually attracted to live in the 5th and 8th Houses as well. The 7th House strictly looks at our approach to partnership and merging with others.

The 7th House shows us that the quality of our relationships can enhance our lives and our sense of self in many ways, but also, it can show us the darker side of what our unions may look like. This is something seldomly mentioned regarding the 7th House, but our public enemies tend to "live" in the 7th House in our charts.

We experience 7th House profection years at ages 6, 18, 30, 42, 54, 66, 78, 90, and 102. During these years, our focus shifts to our relationships and themes of merging with others. As always, we can look to the ruler of the sign on the 7th House cusp, its placement in the chart, and relevant transits for more specific information around what a specific profection year holds for us

The planets are the "doers" in a chart. So, a chart with many planets in the 7th House indicates that the person focuses quite a bit of energy on their partnerships with others. Planets in the 7th House can also clue us in to the crucial attributes related to how we cooperate (or not) within our relationships.

TAROT (IRL)
LIBRA - JUSTICE

The Justice card almost universally features scales in the imagery. The two sides of the scales represent the blend of spirituality/intuition and intellect/logic.

When the Justice card shows up, it points to a number of Libra themes. It can be a time in our lives when we're going through a difficult situation that feels unfair in some way. The Justice card shows us that things keep a balance on their own. The universe often has a way of "evening up the score."

Justice can also show up in these challenging instances to prompt us to examine our relationship to cause/effect and accountability. When we're in a tough situation, the Justice card can show up to ask us, "What was your part in this thing?" Of course, this doesn't mean that every undesirable thing that happens to us is our fault somehow. But, in many instances, humans can struggle with taking accountability for situations they had a hand in creating. Justice reminds us that owning our shit is critical for creating balance in our lives.

We also frequently see the Justice card when things are out of balance in our lives in some way. It's a call to pay close attention to areas where we may be overdoing things and important areas where we might be more neglectful. In terms of relationship spreads, it can show us that our relationships are good and balanced, especially with the card in the upright position, surrounded by cards echoing positive, balanced themes. On the other hand, it can also show us when we're giving or taking within our relationships in an unbalanced way. This is true of the reversal and/or having the Justice card surrounded by other cards in the spread tied to themes of selfishness, selflessness, etc.

THE PAGE OF SWORDS - CARDINAL AIR

Who is the Page of Swords? This page is loosely aligned with Cardinal Air energy. They're an air and earth combo. It's also youthful energy. They feel young, fresh, and inexperienced - smart and curious, yet still in the process of getting a grasp on the earthly aspects of their skills.

This is the essence of fresh airy baby energy. There's a lot of mental energy zipping around. Like all the pages, its gift is that it hasn't yet experienced the heaviness and rigidity that comes with maturity. The world has a particular way of molding our thoughts into conformity. But, this page is still open to all the possibilities, however unrealistic. It's a burst of fresh innovation. Instead of working within the confines of what already exists, it prefers to propose and create new and unprecedented solutions. When met with nay-saying, this page says, "why not?" This is the kind of fresh thinking that brings innovation into the tangible world.

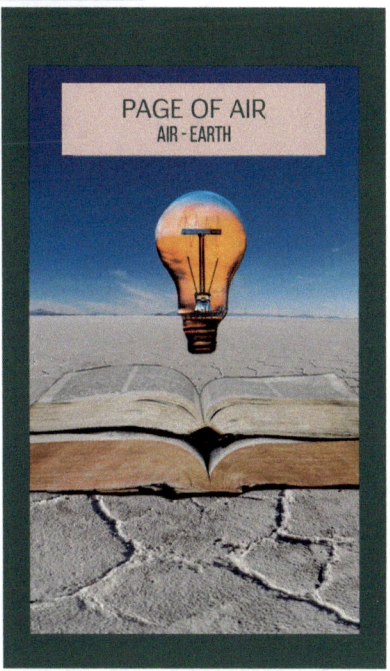

The Page of Swords is also interested in gaining its footing where communication is concerned. It's chatty and inquisitive. There's a love of research and debate present in this page. It's just excited to explore all of the fresh possibility in the world.

However, as with all of the pages, there is a certain sense of naivety which can lead to negligence. We can't know what we don't know, and as curious as this page is, there's a lot it doesn't know. Not all of its innovative ideas may be thoroughly thought out, but this is how we learn. In terms of communication, this page may also lack the weight or effect their words have out in the world. So, there can be unintentional damage to relationships stemming from inexperience. But, one thing is for sure. When this page shows up, it's time to deep-dive into new ideas!

THE KING OF SWORDS - CARDINAL AIR

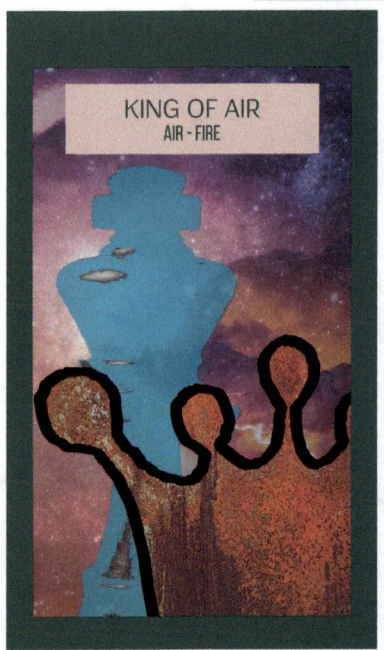

The King of Swords is aligned with Cardinal Air Energy in the court. The King of Swords is elder air energy - air on fire. This king represents the mature ability to reason, strategize, and solve problems with integrity.

We're thinking clearly in the King of Swords, and we understand that our thoughts and actions hold great rewards and/or consequences. So there's a certain level of care and accountability in this king.

When the King of Swords shows up in a reading, it's a sign that we need to focus in on the truth and use it responsibly. The air/fire blend present in this king shows a sense of heart and consideration for others in its ability to analyze, strategize, and reason. This king may not always be an innovator, but it knows how to use its knowledge and experience to make tried and true decisions. The King of Swords is graced with a clear mind and knows how to peer deeply into situations from all angles and consider potential courses of action before making a move. The image that always comes to mind is a master chess player. It's about always thinking moves ahead.

The King of Swords also understands that while compassionate judgment is essential, making decisions when we're in overly-emotional spaces can have some reasonably significant consequences, a lesson many of us have learned the hard way. So this king urges us to be empathetic, impartial, and level-headed when we're faced with something we need to reason through.

The last thing we have to talk about is this king's sense of personal authority. When we're in a King of Swords space, we have a firm grasp on our sense of agency. Every action is rooted in our knowledge and lived experience.

MEET THE COURT (IRL)
MEET THE PAGE AND KING OF SWORDS (IRL)

Use the camera on your phone to scan the QR code and access blogs where we'll discuss real life examples of the Page and King of Swords.

ARIES SEASON TAROT + JOURNALING PROMPTS
ASK JUSTICE...

These are perfect for Libra Season tarot inquiries or even as journaling prompts.

WHAT AREAS COULD BE IMPROVED IN MY RELATIONSHIPS?

DOES MY LIFE FEEL BALANCED? IF NOT, WHERE AM I GIVING TOO MUCH OR TOO LITTLE?

WHAT THINGS FEEL UNFAIR TO ME? WHY MIGHT THAT BE?

IN WHAT WAYS DO I PEOPLE PLEASE? WHY MIGHT THIS BE THE CASE?

WHAT UNPRODUCTIVE CYCLES DO I REPEAT IN MY RELATIONSHIPS WITH OTHERS? HOW COULD I WORK ON CHANGING THOSE HABITS?

ACE OF SWORDS - CARDINAL AIR

CONCENTRATION - FOCUS - NEW IDEAS - TRUTH

When we're in this ace, we're experiencing a mental breakthrough. We can see things clearly for the first time in a long time. This ace kicks off a journey through one of the more uncomfortable suits in the minor arcana. The artwork throughout the swords can be pretty gnarly. But, the swords are here to do help us do meaningful work. They're responsible for how we learn to focus our mental efforts and beliefs in the world. They help us find the balance between intellect and power.

This ace represents the start of a mental shift, typically one that will benefit us long-term. Although we may encounter painful or difficult situations along the way, the ultimate goal is growth. It's about adapting the way we think to better function in the world. This ace presents us with that fresh opportunity to get the ball rolling.

2 OF SWORDS - MOON IN LIBRA

DIFFICULT CHOICES - CONFUSION - STALEMATE

After becoming aware of a necessary mental shift in the Ace of Swords, we find ourselves in the 2. Here, we understand that there are choices to be made related to the new information we've discovered in the ace.

However, we might feel stuck between where we once were and where we know we're going. It can be a struggle to step out of our comfort zone. We can be in denial or feel like we don't have all the necessary information.

The figure on the 2 of Swords is typically blindfolded and holds two swords crossed in front of them, creating a sort of boundary. This shows us that we may feel vulnerable and need boundaries and protection during this time. The blindfold represents that as much as we might like to be able to see the outcome. No one can see the future. Sometimes we simply have to do what we feel/know is right and trust that the result will be what we need.

3 OF SWORDS - SATURN IN LIBRA

HEARTBREAK - PAIN - UPSET

After making difficult choices in the 2 of Swords, we find ourselves in the 3. The imagery often shows a heart with 3 swords piercing through it as storm clouds brew in the background.

People often wonder why a "heartbreak" card is found within the suit of swords rather than the cups. When we make difficult decisions and experience loss, it's emotional. But there's also a mental component. We have to process the hurt. We have to think logically about it and get our heads and hearts on the same page. It's also a mental process to learn from the things that have hurt us. This knowledge helps us to make better decisions in the future. So, as much as we all hate feeling like shit, it's a necessary part of the human experience. Without it, we wouldn't be able to grow or appreciate the good things in life. These upsets provide us a sense of perspective and gratitude.

4 OF SWORDS - JUPITER IN LIBRA

REST - RELAXATION - RECUPERATION

Up to this point, we've done some hard work in the ace, 2, and 3, and we find ourselves in the 4. Making these significant changes weighs on us. There can be a lot of mental strain and sleepless nights. The energy of Jupiter (opportunity) meets up with Libra in the 4 of Swords and reminds us to rest.

These are the periods where we need to hole up in our rooms, disconnect from the outside world, binge our favorite show, and just...relax. The human stress response isn't meant to be a space where we spend prolonged periods of time. We require time to recharge, especially as we head further into the swords to continue our journey.

Existing in productivity-obsessed late-stage capitalism can make this a challenging card for many people. Rest requires a certain level of privilege that not all of us have access to. But, it is a basic human need.

LIBRA SEASON ACTIVITY
PERCEPTION PRECEDES REALITY

Andy Warhol once said that "perception precedes reality," and we know that charming Venusian Libra cares about how it's perceived. We live in a world where opinions can be rapidly-shared and regarded as fact, no matter how true or untrue they may be. Unfortunately, we also live in a world where our self-image can be warped by messaging all around us. There are entire industries and societal structures which benefit from ensuring that many of us keep our self-image small. So, there's often a divide or an imbalance between how we perceive ourselves and how others perceive us. This is a Libra Season Activity to attempt to close this gap and help us get a more balanced view of how we feel we show up in the world versus how we actually show up in the world.

I'm sure we've all seen a word cloud at some point, and that's what we're going to be doing. First, list 20 words that you think are accurate descriptors for yourself. Be honest with yourself. How do you think of yourself? Next, make a list of 20 words that you think other people would use to describe you.

Now, you're going to solicit feedback from others. Reach out to your friends, family, acquaintances, and co-workers and ask them for the one-word descriptor they would assign to you. An easy way to do this is to put a poll in your social media stories. I did this when I was testing out this activity, and it worked well. Your stories archive will even compile all the responses in one place for you.

Once you have all the responses, you can feed them into a word cloud generator online. Tons of free websites can generate one for you. Make sure you enter any duplicate words. The generators will make those words bigger in the cloud. Once your word cloud is generated, compare it against the two lists of descriptors you made. How does the word cloud stack up? Would the scale be balanced if we were to place our descriptors on one side of a scale and the words generated by others on the other side? Generally speaking, the people who have tried this found that they are far more critical of themselves than they should be. Another helpful activity would be to make a stylized version of the word cloud and keep it somewhere where you will see it daily. Let it be a reminder that our perceptions are not always valid. Thoughts and feelings are not always reflective of reality.

KITCHEN WITCHIN'
FRIENDSGIVING - BOOZY APPLE CIDER SANGRIA

We all know that witch bitches start jonesing for fall flavors in like...August. So, here's a great autumn sangria recipe perfect for sharing with friends!

INGREDIENTS
- apples (I like to use Honeycrisp, but any variety will do)
- pears
- plums
- cinnamon sticks
- 1 bottle pinot grigio
- apple cider
- club soda
- bourbon
- maple syrup (optional)

INSTRUCTIONS

You'll notice there are no quantities listed for a number of these ingredients. This is because Sangria should be made to taste! Everyone likes something different! (Yes, I'm forcing you to make decisions during Libra Season...)

1) Fill your pitcher a third of the way with chunks of fruit. You can leave the skins on. The fruit will soften, so start with firmer fruit if you can. Next, add cinnamon sticks (as many as you like).

2) Add an entire bottle of pinot grigio, a few cups of apple cider, some club soda, and bourbon. Everything is to taste. You can add maple syrup if you desire extra sweetness. Stir everything up!

3) Place in the refrigerator and allow it to sit for 2 hours. After two hours, give it a stir, and serve!

PRACTICAL MAGICK
IF YOU WANNA BE MY LOVER, YOU GOTTA GET WITH MY FRIENDS

We all know that Libra season is all about relationships. I grew up in the early 90s, which could perhaps be considered the golden era of tacky DIY best friend jewelry. This was a fave late summer/early fall camp craft. It's affordable, creative, and keeps the hands busy, which is excellent for stress relief. I vote we bring them back, with a witchy twist, of course. Scan the QR code below, and let's make some Libra Season Magick, friends!

LIBRA SEASON FRIENDSHIP BRACELET MAGICK
Use your phone's camera to scan the QR code & access this content.

LIBRA SEASON WORDS: THE TAKEAWAY
ALL THINGS IN MODERATION, KID

We leave Virgo season with our lives (hopefully) in order and having done some serious solo introspection. Libra Season urges us to get back out there and start socializing again. But it's always about balance where Libra is concerned. It's like my dad always says to me, "all things in moderation, kid."

The season brings a certain level of "treat yourself" energy. It's Venusian, after all. But, it's more than just buying yourself everything on your online wishlist. Libra isn't selfish. It cares about social justice and the underdog, and it understands that we have to take care of ourselves to be able to show up for others. There's a balance that has to be struck between focusing on the self and focusing on the not-self.

It's also a time to fine-tune our relationships. We spent time in Virgo Season working on ourselves. But, Libra Season reminds us to put that same amount of effort into our relationships with others. Relationships are a lesson in give and take, and Libra Season is a time to explore that.

The Libra/Aries polarity is all about this idea of defining ourselves. The Aries side of the polarity is self-interested. It's about defining ourselves as individuals. The Libra side of the polarity is interested in defining and examining the sense of self through the lens of others' perceptions and expectations. Both are important and needed in moderation. Being too self-centered isolates us from the collective human experience. Conversely, allowing ourselves to be exclusively defined by others robs us of our sense of individual expression. We have to find the middle.

If we were to draw a Venn Diagram of "who are we when we're alone" and "who are we when we're in the company of others," the hope is that there's a substantial overlap in the center. That's what we aim for in Libra Season and in life. Of course, we all have parts of ourselves that are reserved for just us. We also have roles we play out in society that we may not whole-heartedly identify with. But, the idea is that we've found a balance that allows us to frequently feel autonomy in how we've defined ourselves as individuals and that garners us authentic acceptance in our relationships.

LIBRA

A perfectly set table -
> Hand-written thank you notes. (Who says etiquette is dead?)

Fusion -
> The process of combining two or more distinct entities into a new singular entity. (Alexa, play 2 Become 1 by the Spice Girls.)

A right hand raised -
> "Do you swear to tell the truth, the whole truth, and nothing but the truth?" (Well, do you?)

I'm fine -
> "I'm not mad." (Passive aggression as a love language.)

Online shopping sprees -
> Skincare, clothing, jewelry...for serotonin. How else will we keep the economy alive? (Just doing my part.)

"Omg, did you hear?" -
> "Well, a cousin of their friend told me..." (Gossip as a bonding activity.)

Pinterest boards -
> Craft blogs. (DIY Darling.)

Rom-Coms -
> In love with being in love. (Noah screaming at Allie, "What do you want?" - such a vibe.)

I need your help. I can't decide -
> Outfit A or B? (Let's take a vote.)

Ok, but seriously -
> What do YOU want to eat? (I'm really fine with anything...)

Practicing a response over and over in the mirror -
> Performance reviews and difficult conversations are THE WORST (Directness is overrated.)

Cher's father, in shock -
> "You mean to tell me you argued your way from a C+ to an A-" (Totally based on my powers of persuasion.)

Best friend bracelets -
> Secrets exchanged at sleepovers. ("I've never told anyone this before...")

What will they think of me?
> Does it really matter? (What do YOU think of you?)

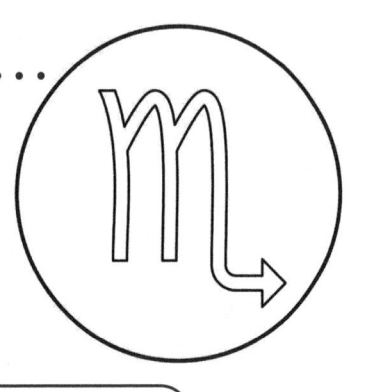

SCORPIO

- **DATES:** OCTOBER 23 - NOVEMBER 21
- **ELEMENT:** WATER
- **MODALITY:** FIXED
- **RULING PLANET:** PLUTO + MARS
- **HOUSE:** EIGHTH
- **PHRASE:** I TRANSFORM
- **GLYPH:** THE SCORPION, THE EAGLE, THE PHOENIX
- **TAROT CARDS:** 5 OF CUPS, 6 OF CUPS, 7 OF CUPS, QUEEN OF CUPS, DEATH, AND, JUDGMENT

SCORPIO SEASON PLAYLIST

USE THE CAMERA APP ON YOUR PHONE TO ACCESS THIS PLAYLIST.

SCORPIO - A BRIEF INTRODUCTION

Alright, witches, it's Scorpio Season. You know what that means...spooky season is here! The Cardinal Air of Libra Season kicked off fall, and now the Fixed Water of Scorpio Season is here to settle us into those incredible spooky vibes!

This is the time of year when we start to see the changing leaves dry up and fall. It's getting colder, and much of the plant life around us is dying. The days are getting shorter. The sky is darker, and it's time to explore all the mysterious and unseen things.

Historically speaking, this would be the time of year when the harvest and preparation work for the coming winter is largely complete. So, we have a little more time on our hands. I know this is difficult for us to fathom, living in modern-day Capitalism where most of us work fixed timeframes regardless of the time of year. But, historically speaking, workloads ebbed and flowed. So, there would be busy times (like Virgo Season) and more restful times (like Scorpio Season), and this time would often be used for deep reflection.

As humans watch nature dying all around them, there's always been some awareness of connecting with the dead during this time of year. Cultures worldwide and throughout human history celebrate this season as a "thinning of the veil." Scorpio Season reminds us that death is part of the cycle. As plants die, there's an understanding that they will grow back in the spring. Just because we can't see the seeds doing their work under the surface doesn't mean they're not there. It also touches on the idea of death and rebirth, which are both common Scorpio themes. It's like they say, "Only two things in life are certain: death and taxes." (We'll discuss taxes and shared wealth later in this section when we cover the 8th House.)

I certainly don't need to tell a group of witches this, but it's also Halloween. Aside from scooping up all the best "seasonal" decor (to be used year-round), it's a time of year dedicated to facing our fears, examining the darker and more shadowy parts of ourselves, and allowing ourselves to be transformed by that knowledge. If it sounds like a season of intensity, that's because it is. This is one of the significant hallmarks of the Scorpio archetype.

So, get your scary movie queue ready...it's Scorpio Season!

SCORPIO (IRL)

The Scorpio/Taurus polarity shares wealth, resource management, and power themes. On the Taurus side of things, we're focused on material wealth, having, the power than comes with an abundance of tangible resources, and the experience of existing in a physical body. On the other hand, Scorpio's half of the polarity covers shared wealth and resources (taxes/inheritance), non-material wealth (expressed as power and authority), and the act of releasing our physical bodies (AKA, death).

Pluto rules Scorpio in the modern rulership model. If you're into mythology, you know that Pluto was the ruler of the underworld and afterlife, and Scorpio is very much rooted in "underworld" themes. Anyone who was "anyone" in mythology did their stint in the underworld and came back a badder bitch for it. So, it's no surprise that Scorpio is universally tied to death, rebirth, and transformation.

When we think about what this looks like in our day-to-day life, we have to think about all the moments in our lives that really "changed" us. Typically, those moments are big and intense (and not very easy). Scorpio/Pluto energy feels a lot like being in a pressure cooker. The archetypes are known to apply the necessary pressure in our lives required for change. Is it comfy? No. But does that pressure release feel great when our transformational work is done? Hell yes. (You're totally picturing an InstantPot, aren't you?) But seriously, Scorpio's work is often a big lesson in human resiliency. In fact, Scorpio is one of the only zodiac signs to have multiple symbols/glyphs representing it. Most people are familiar with the scorpion, but it's also characterized by a phoenix. I think we're all familiar with the imagery of a phoenix rising from the ashes. (No additional explanation needed, right?)

Scorpio is known for exploring deep truths, and it doesn't care how pretty they are. It just wants the truth in its rawest form. It's imperative is to bring things out of the dark into the light. It's THE detective of the zodiac. While Scorpio is very skilled at figuring out what makes someone/something tick (heavily Scorpio folks make great therapists, by the way), it can also bring on a certain level of secrecy, judgment, obsession, and manipulation. Remember, Scorpio is interested in power exchanges. So, we have to take the good with the not-so-good. But, honestly, this is the case with the entire zodiac. In the end, Scorpio Season is the ultimate time for shadow work, boundary work, and deep reflection.

MEET PLUTO

Pluto rules Scorpio in the modern rulership model. Mars is its traditional ruler. Here's the thing. We didn't always know that Uranus, Neptune, and Pluto were there. They weren't discovered until after the 1700s. So, some signs have two rulers, one modern and one traditional.

Pluto has a massive 248-year orbit. So, we'll never experience a personal Pluto Return (I mean, unless we're a vampire or something). Pluto spends roughly 20 years in each sign. This means that everyone born within those 20 years would have the same Pluto sign, generationally speaking. The sign would be a sort of "generational stamp." But, where it would be personally expressed in each individual would be determined by the house it falls within, as that differs from person to person.

In astrology, signs are like adjectives or adverbs. They describe "how" a planet will act. The houses represent the "where," as in what area of life. I look at it like this. Whatever house your Pluto falls within is where you're an agent working on behalf of Pluto. Mine is in the 3rd House (The House of Communication). So, I would be a "mouthpiece" for Pluto. You get the idea.

Generationally speaking, Pluto represents what a generation transforms and what truths it brings to light. For example, if you're a Gen X'r, you would very likely be Pluto in Libra. This generation transformed aesthetics, relationships, and social groups. If you're a Millennial, you're probably Pluto in Scorpio. We're responsible for uncovering and shining a light on dark, unspoken truths (think about the Me Too Movement, BLM, etc.). These aren't new problems. We're just responsible for bringing them to light. Finally, if you're a member of Gen Z, you probably have Pluto in Sagittarius. Your generation is tasked with transforming the dogma and bureaucracy associated with outdated government, religious, and philosophical structures.

On a personal level, Pluto in our birth charts represents the area of life where we bring truth to the forefront and how we search for deeper meaning in life. It also shows us where we hold personal power and have the most significant transformational potential. Last, it represents where we may encounter power struggles and even a sense of obsession or manipulation in our lives.

IT'S JUST A PHASE...
SCORPIO SEASON MOONS (IRL)

During Scorpio Season, we typically experience a Scorpio New Moon and a Taurus Full Moon.

SCORPIO NEW MOON

The Scorpio New Moon is a time for stepping into our personal power as well as shadow work and reflection. First, we have to remember that Scorpio is Fixed Water energy. So, it's not uncommon for deeply buried emotions to surface. Many shadowy themes such as our fears and insecurities may bubble up to the surface. Most of the time we keep this stuff bottled up so that we can be functional out in the world. But, we all have a dark side, and the Scorpio New Moon kicks off a period where we're meant to acknowledge and examine those parts of ourselves. Our unique source of power and drive can often be found in that work. (We can't forget that Scorpio's traditional ruler is Mars, the planet of drive.) This new moon is beneficial as a catalyst for the significant changes we wish to make in our lives. Because if there's one thing we know about Scorpio/Pluto/Mars energy, it never does anything halfway. It loves to live on the extremes.

TAURUS FULL MOON

The Taurus Full Moon arrives during Scorpio Season to remind us of the other half of the Scorpio/Taurus Polarity. With all the focus on death, shadow work, and transformation that comes with the season, the Taurus Full Moon reminds us to "be here now." It's a reminder that we are in a body existing on the physical plane and that we need to make the most of it while we're here because, as Scorpio Season teaches us...life is short, and no one is here forever. However, if we're constantly caught up in Plutonian intensity, we can forget to enjoy the sensual pleasures all around us. This is an excellent time to enjoy a favorite meal, listen to your favorite music, buy yourself that thing you've had in your online shopping cart for ages, take a nap, or get a massage. You get the idea. It's about doing something that pulls you out of your deep mental and emotional reflection and connects you with your body and the physical world in the here and now. Frankly, this is necessary to ease us out of the depths of Scorpio Season and allow us some time during the waning moon period to recalibrate before an expansive Sagittarius Season.

WELCOME HOME
THE 8TH HOUSE (IRL) - THE HOUSE OF TRANSFORMATION

In a natural chart, Scorpio is associated with the 8th House, and it's often referred to as the "House of Transformation." It's one of my favorite houses, but perhaps I'm biased...

The 8th House has a lot going on. It is where death, sex, other people's money, taxes, inheritance, the occult, personal power, and transformation live. At first glance, I know this feels like a strange mash-up of subjects, but there is an organizing theme here. Everything on this list is invisible and/or taboo in modern culture. This is all the stuff that we do and deal with, but we don't often openly talk about. I once had an astrologer I admire tell me during a reading that, historically speaking, 8th House people were the "guardians between worlds," meaning they were often birth or death doulas. They could communicate with the living and the dead. They were sort of behind-the-scenes organizers for collective transformation. Today, the best examples we have are therapists and death industry workers. But as more and more people explore modern spirituality, we see a return to some of the more traditional 8th House roles that once existed in the public eye. You can always tell when you're dealing with an 8th House heavy person if you ask, "Do you want to see/hear something weird?" The answer will always be yes.

The planets are the "doers" in a chart. So, when we see a chart with many planets in the 8th House, we have someone dedicating quite a bit of their energy to sex, death, the occult, magick, transformation, and power exchange in the world.

Outside of natal planets in the 8th House, transits to our 8th House and 8th House profection years help us continually evolve and refine how we deal with our sense of all the 8th House themes mentioned here. We experience 8th House profection years at ages 7, 19, 31, 43, 55, 67, 79, 91, and 103. As always, we can look to the ruler of the sign on the 8th House cusp, its placement in the chart, and relevant transits for more specific information around what a specific profection year holds for us. So take a look at your 8th House. What would you say is your attitude toward life's "taboos"? What does it tell you about your relationship to intensity and power exchange?

TAROT (IRL)
SCORPIO - DEATH

Scorpio is associated with the Death card in the Major Arcana. It's true what they say. "The only two things that are certain in life are death and taxes." The thing about life is that none of us will get out alive. Everything about our existence is finite, including the space in our lives. This means we can't (and shouldn't) do or have it all. To make space for new things and facilitate personal growth, we have to release the things that are no longer serving us. We have to create room in our lives for new people, places, and experiences.

People often confuse Death card energy and Tower card energy. There is good reason for this. The two do feel similar. Scorpio's traditional ruler is Mars. Scorpio represents Death card energy, and Mars represents Tower card energy. Both cards involve releasing something that isn't working for us anymore. But, there is a critical difference. There is a conscious quality in the letting go associated with the Death card.

Where the Tower represents the moments in life where the universe removes something that we wouldn't ordinarily be inclined to let go of on our own, the Death card actively involves our sense of personal agency.

This doesn't mean that Death card work is always comfortable. It simply implies we're choosing the discomfort because we know we need to make space for what's coming next. This card often reminds me of a break-up where both parties care about one another, but they know it's just not working. They see the split as inevitable, and eventually, they choose the separation. It won't mean that the break-up will be easy. But, they know that finally, they will both find something that is a better fit.

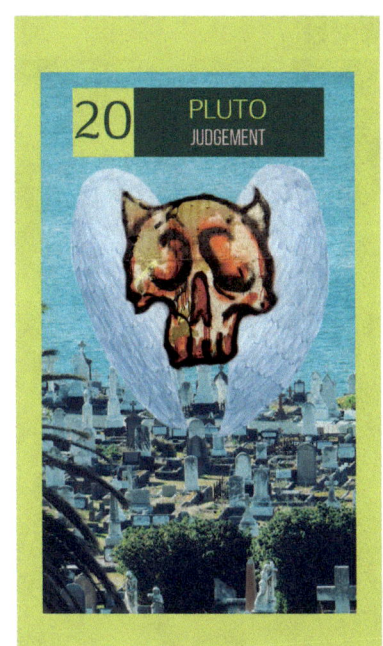

PLUTO - JUDGMENT

Scorpio's modern ruler, Pluto, is associated with the Judgment card in the Major Arcana.

We haven't talked about "The Fool's Journey" yet, since the Fool will be covered in the Aquarius section. But, when we consider the entire Major Arcana, The Fool represents pure potential. It's kind of like a baby in utero. It exists and doesn't yet exist all at the same time. So, from The Magician through The World, the sequential Major Arcana represents a complete cycle of growth and learning, which we often refer to as "The Fool's Journey." We cycle through the Major Arcana repeatedly throughout our lives as we learn different lessons. As soon as we wrap up a lesson in The World, we jump right back in at The Fool to learn something new. This is how we grow.

Judgment is the second to the last card in the Major Arcana. It's followed only by The World card, and it represents the moments of reflection, reckoning, and evaluation as we approach the end of a given cycle.

The artwork for this card typically depicts a scene of the living and dead being summoned to their judgment. This is a period of taking inventory and integrating all of the lessons we've learned in our Fool's Journey. It's a moment of honest appraisal where we become keenly aware of our growth. Pluto rules transformation, after all.

There's also an aspect of this card that recognizes the "bigger picture" in the interconnectedness of all things. Our understanding of the world is that everything we can perceive is made up of atoms and the space between those atoms. So, where does one thing end and another thing begin? When we think about it like this, the boundaries become blurred. So, when we're judging someone else, what we're really judging is ourselves. Because, in the end, who's really to say where they end and we begin?

THE QUEEN OF CUPS - FIXED WATER

Who is the Queen of Cups? This queen is aligned with Fixed Water energy. It's a double water combo, elementally speaking, and it feels exactly as you might expect.

The Queen of Cups is compassionate and nurturing. This archetype is empathy embodied. It understands the emotions behind what motivates people, and it can hold space for its own feelings and the feelings of others like no other.

This queen always feels like "grandma" energy. There's always a sensitive piece of wisdom to be offered (along with a bomb plate of homemade cookies.)

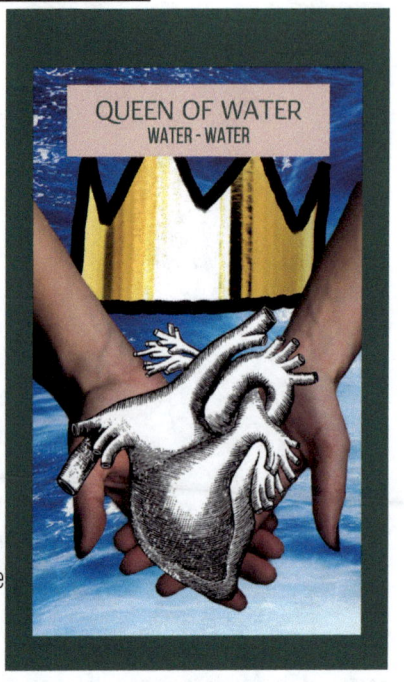

QUEEN OF WATER
WATER - WATER

The Queen of Cups is the "emotional rock" within all of us. It's able to see our full potential and gently encourage us, even when we can't seem to see it in ourselves. It's very much the vibe of the parent in the front row at all of your childhood plays and sporting events, obsessively snapping photos. This queen is, without a doubt, the archetype that teaches us all about self-love and self-acceptance.

There's also a deep intuition present with this queen. (You're shocked. I know.) The archetype feels almost a little "High Priestess Lite." It thinks with its heart first. Feelings color all thoughts, and when we're in a Queen of Cups space, our gut feelings about things are often spot-on. That being said, this archetype can lack basic common sense from time to time. But, I suppose that's to be expected when emotions are the priority.

When the Queen of Cups visits us, we're being asked to suspend our busy minds and feel into the emotional needs of ourselves and those around us.

MEET THE COURT (IRL)
MEET THE QUEEN OF CUPS (IRL)

Use the camera on your phone to scan the QR code and access blogs where we'll discuss real life examples of the Queen of Cups.

THE MINOR ARCANA
5 OF CUPS - MARS IN SCORPIO

LOSS - REGRET - GRIEF

I once saw a guy with two cups tattooed on the backs of his upper arms. I approached him and asked, "Is that a 5 of Cups tattoo?" He was so excited. I don't think many people get the reference. But what a clever tattoo...

The 5 of Cups depicts a person looking deeply upset while facing 3 tipped-over cups. Behind them are two upright cups. (Get the tattoo reference now?)

Like all 5's, we're experiencing some less than pleasant emotions in the 5 of Cups. Loss and grief are a part of life. The finite nature of our existence is the very thing that makes it so special. Often, we have to feel what it is to lose something to truly appreciate what we have.

Also, and this is important, nothing is forever. If this person were to turn around, they would see that they still have 2 upright cups right behind them. They just couldn't see them because they were so focused on the 3 tipped-over cups in front of them. The same is often true in life.

131

6 OF WANDS - SUN IN SCORPIO

NOSTALGIA - MEMORIES - FAMILIAR THINGS

After experiencing a loss in the 5 of Cups, we can be understandably nostalgic for what once was. This is the energy of the 6 of Cups.

It's like listening to an old mixed tape or smelling a familiar smell that transports us back to a distinct memory. There can be comfort in remembering the past. We are a collection of our lived experiences. Our memories are what make us.

But, science also shows that our memories can be unreliable. We can don our rose-colored glasses and remember things, not as they were, but as we wanted them to be. Memories are simply stories we tell ourselves.

It's ok to remember where we've come from, but it's challenging to move forward in our lives if we're constantly looking backward.

7 OF WANDS - VENUS IN SCORPIO

CHOICES - ILLUSION - INDECISION

After spending time in the nostalgia of the 6 of Cups, we're ready to move forward in the 7 of Cups. The problem is, we don't know which path to choose. Instructions unclear. A little help, please...

The artwork for the 7 of Cups typically pictures a person standing before 7 cups. Each cup is filled with something different. Some cups appear to be filled with promise for the future. Others hold danger. The basic premise: We have all the choices at our disposal, but not all choices are choices that will be good for us.

It's a card about choosing wisely. In the 7 of Cups, we need to be aware of wishful thinking. We have to balance our emotions with an objective review of the options. It's a great time to make a pros and cons list and think about the advantages and disadvantages of each choice. Of course, we can never know the outcome, but we must do our due diligence.

PRACTICAL MAGICK
SHADOW WORK IS THE NEW BLACK - A TAROT SPREAD

If you exist in any spiritual social media spaces, you've no doubt heard of the concept of shadow work. The term stem's from Carl Jung's theory of a "shadow self." Essentially, the shadow self represents the "less desirable" and darker traits within us - jealousy, anger, etc. Jung theorized that if we don't acknowledge our shadow, it will make its presence in our life more prominent and more destructive. The idea behind shadow work is to recognize and accept all parts of ourselves (even the dark parts).

ME AND MY SHADOW

Use your phone's camera to scan the QR code & access this bonus content.

SCORPIO SEASON TAROT + JOURNALING PROMPTS
ASK DEATH + JUDGMENT...

These prompts are perfect for Scorpio Season tarot or even as journaling prompts.

WHAT ARE MY MOST "UNDESIRABLE" QUALITIES?

WHAT MAKES ME FEEL POWERFUL? WHAT MAKES ME FEEL POWERLESS? WHY?

WHAT ARE MY THOUGHTS AROUND DEATH AND DYING?

WHAT MAKES ME FEEL JEALOUS OR POSSESSIVE? WHY MIGHT THAT BE?

HOW DO I DEAL WITH ENDINGS?

KITCHEN WITCHIN'
PUMPKIN SLUT

Scorpio Season is horror movie season in our house. It's also all-things-pumpkin season. (Yes, I'm one of "those" pumpkin sluts.) These vegan, no-bake pumpkin balls are the perfect movie-time snack to check all the boxes. Recipe yields 16.

NO BAKE PUMPKIN BALLS

INSTRUCTIONS

1) Place the raisins in a bowl and cover them with hot water. Allow them to soak there for approximately 10 minutes, and then drain.

2) Place the raisins and nuts in a food processor and pulse until they've formed a paste.

3) Next, add the pumpkin puree, coconut flakes, vanilla, and spices to the blender. Pulse a few times until everything is well-combined.

4) Place the mixture in the refrigerator for a minimum of 30 minutes.

5) Remove the mixture from the refrigerator, and divide it into 16 portions. Roll each piece into a ball, and they're ready to eat!

(These can be stored in an airtight container in the refrigerator for up to 5 days.)

INGREDIENTS

- 1 cup raisins
- 1/2 cup pecans or cashews
- 1/2 cup unsweetened coconut flakes
- 2 tsp vanilla
- 1 tsp cinnamon
- 1/4 tsp nutmeg
- 1/4 tsp ground cloves

DEATH IS A PART OF LIFE
(SO, WHY DOES NO ONE TALK ABOUT?)

Death avoidance is a relatively new phenomenon in Western Culture. Inflation has made everything more expensive. Most households need to be dual-income to stay afloat. With two people working, it's not often possible for someone to be home to provide care for elderly relatives. As a result, they're usually hidden away in nursing homes or hospitals in their final years.

We've distanced ourselves from death. Maybe on purpose, maybe not. But, funerals are now referred to as "celebrations of life," and we've normalized euphemisms like "passed away" as opposed to saying "someone died." Bodies of the deceased are pumped with chemicals and made up to look like they're still alive, just sleeping. But it wasn't always this way...

Even as recently as the 1800s, funerals were held in the homes of the deceased. There was rarely embalming. This was a relatively new development that resulted from the Civil War. It enabled the bodies of dead soldiers to be shipped back to Europe. But for most people who died during this era, the deceased's body was publicly displayed in the home for the public to come and pay their respects. Family and loved ones would sit with the body for days. This stemmed from a belief that watching over the body protects against evil spirits. It was also to ensure that the person was actually dead and didn't wake up. This is where we get the terminology of a "wake." This is also where the term "living room" originated. Living rooms were previously referred to as "parlors." But, as more funerals began taking place in funeral homes in the late 19th century, the family parlors used once to display the dead bodies started being referred to as "living rooms" since this is where the living would now congregate.

Death photography was also a norm. Portraits of the deceased were taken and hung in the family home. This served as a reminder that everything and everyone who lives will eventually die. Death existed in plain sight. It was a part of everyday culture. People were closer to death. It served as a reminder of our finite nature, which is what makes everything we experience in our time here so special. If you haven't spent much time considering and planning for your own death, Scorpio Season is an ideal time to do it. Explore funeral options. Ask yourself what you might like to have done with your body...because none of us will get out alive.

SCORPIO SEASON WORDS: THE TAKEAWAY
DEATH MAY BE THE GREATEST OF ALL HUMAN BLESSINGS

Socrates is quoted as saying, "Death may be the greatest of all human blessings." So, what did he mean by that? The quote comes from Plato's The Apology, an account of Socrates' speech at his trial for not recognizing the gods as the state required. The formal charges were "impiety and corrupting the youth," and he was obviously sentenced to death. The entire trail is filled with Scorpio/Judgment Card themes, a battle of wills between a curious truth-teller and the inflexible powers that be, which ultimately results in a death sentence carried out by forced hemlock ingestion. (Hemlock is often associated with Scorpio.)

Socrates basically reasons to the jury that he's okay with capital punishment. He says that death is either complete annihilation (like a deep and restful sleep) or transmigration (where the soul goes on to live somewhere else). He states that neither option should be something we fear.

I think a fear of death, or at the very least a curiosity about it, is a normal part of being part of a species that is keenly aware of its own mortality. That's a gift and a curse. Knowing that we're going to die is what makes us feel intensely and take risks - YOLO, right? It makes us cherish the things, people, and experiences in our lives because we always know that we're not going to be here forever somewhere in our minds. But also, death is the final frontier, the great unknown...and our conscious minds are somewhat conditioned to fear the unknown. Our brains are tasked with keeping us alive and safe. So, it's a classic Catch-22.

Even on a smaller and less life-and-death scale, quitting a job, letting a friendship fizzle, making a big relocation, or even getting a divorce are endings that cause many of us to feel some valid discomfort. In the end, something better usually comes out of it, and if not, these situations show us what we're made of. Pluto is known for testing our resiliency. It's in these moments that we have the most transformational power. Endings and our personal evolution go hand in hand. We don't benefit from personal growth without the discomfort of learning to let some things go. Everything runs its course. Nothing is forever. The premise of endings is central to Scorpio Season. But are they really endings? Or are they just part of a larger cycle of growth and transformation?

SCORPIO

Jack O'Lanterns Glowing -
    Irish lore. Stingy Jack, the drunkard, making a deal with the devil and being doomed to roam the Earth with only a hollowed turnip to light his way. (It always starts with a deal with the devil, doesn't it? When will mortals learn?)

The familiar crater in your therapist's couch -
    "So, tell me about your mother…" Instant intimacy. I guess we're jumping right in then… (TBH, I've always hated small-talk anyway.)

The dissonance of string instruments in horror movies -
    Unresolved melodies communicate a sense of urgency to the primal parts of our brains. (Everyone knows that you run out the front door when a killer is chasing you, not upstairs. But I guess she's just not "final girl" material…)

A true-crime podcast hyper fixation -
    In the shower, in the car, at work…(If anyone can solve the Jon Benet Ramsey case, it's me.)

A pressure cooker clicking as the atmosphere inside reaches 15 psi -
    Its contents ready to be subjected to intense pressure and heat. No one said transformation would be comfortable. (But, think of the release…)

Old Cemeteries -
    Above ground: haunting and beautiful. Below ground: bodies becoming worm food. (A reminder that all new life comes from death.)

Credit card statements -
    Tax bills. Debt is power, you know? (It's always nice to have a favor you can call in…)

Sun Tzu's iconic words, "If you know the enemy and you know yourself, you need not fear the result of a hundred battles -"
    So what makes them tick? (Don't get mad, get even.)

The green-eyed monster -
    Like Scorpio Moon, Bette Midler said, "The worst part of success is trying to find someone who is happy for you." (The grass is greener where you water it.)

The eye of a hurricane -
    When you're married to intensity, a certain level of catastrophe is to be expected. (But, like a phoenix from the ashes, you rise - smarter, stronger, and more powerful than before.)

SAGITTARIUS

- **DATES: NOVEMBER 22 - DECEMBER 21**
- **ELEMENT: FIRE**
- **MODALITY: MUTABLE**
- **RULING PLANET: JUPITER**
- **HOUSE: NINTH**
- **PHRASE: I EXPLORE**
- **GLYPH: THE ARCHER**
- **TAROT CARDS: 8 OF WANDS, 9 OF WANDS, 10 OF WANDS, KNIGHT OF WANDS, WHEEL OF FORTUNE, AND TEMPERANCE**

SAGITTARIUS SEASON PLAYLIST
USE THE CAMERA APP ON YOUR PHONE TO ACCESS THIS PLAYLIST.

SAGITTARIUS - A BRIEF INTRODUCTION

As we move through Scorpio Season, we learn about the importance of endings, shared resources, and our relationship to power. Now, as we near the darkest days of the year, Sagittarius offers us the light necessary to see the path that lies ahead. The Mutable Fire energy is here to provide us with a bridge between the Fixed Water of Scorpio Season and the Cardinal Earth energy of Capricorn Season. It's readying us for the last quarter of the astrological year. We're reflecting on lessons we've learned since the preceding Aries Season and determining how we can use that information in the future. It's a time of year filled with celebration and the promise of greater possibilities.

Sagittarius Season was widely regarded as "PTO Season" in my corporate job days. First, there's Thanksgiving (which I don't personally celebrate, but many do). Then the holiday preparation starts for Christmas, Boxing Day, the Winter Solstice, Hanukkah, Kwanzaa, Las Posadas, St. Lucia Day, Three Kings Day, and more. I realize some of these holidays technically occur during Capricorn Season. Still, many of the celebrations leading up to them happen during Sagittarius Season, which makes a lot of sense when you consider what Sagittarius represents as an astrological archetype. We see a season filled with socializing, celebration, rich food and drinks, and holiday traditions. It's all very Sagittarius/Jupiter.

There's a lighter feeling to this time of year. We're less focused on work as the Gregorian calendar winds down. We're more focused on time spent with family and friends, engaging in our various traditions (often tied to spiritual or religious practices). But something interesting I've been thinking about is the connection between Sagittarius Season and consumerism. In Western Culture, this is the time of year when people do a lot of shopping for holiday gifts, often financially over-extending themselves.

Sagittarius/Jupiter energy is often considered generous, perhaps excessively so sometimes. It's also known for "going bigger" and "doing the most," sometimes without regard for consequences. (It is a fire sign, after all.) It's interesting to watch how that plays out regarding things like Black Friday sales and many people going into debt with holiday shopping. Just something of note...astrology can be incredibly literal sometimes.

So, let's get ready to party! It's Sagittarius Season...

SAGITTARIUS (IRL)

Sagittarius is Chiron, the centaur, in Greek Mythology. He was known for teaching medicine, hunting, music, and prophecy. In addition, he was said to be a gifted teacher who taught famous mythological characters Jason and Achilles. This makes sense when considering that Sagittarius, as an archetype, is preoccupied with higher learning and expansion.

When we look at the polarity between Gemini and Sagittarius, curiosity is undoubtedly a prominent theme. Still, the scale of exploration the two signs prefer highlights the critical difference between them. Gemini feels like looking at the world under a microscope. It wants to understand the minutia, nuance, and connection in each thing it explores. On the other hand, Sagittarius is like looking at great expanses of land from the vantage point of being in an airplane. It's interested in "the broad strokes" and "the big picture."

Representing Mutable Fire energy, Sagittarius is known for being friendly, gregarious, larger than life, and full of interesting anecdotes and stories. It's absolutely the storyteller of the zodiac, and it loves to be the most intelligent person in the room. Sagittarius has never met a lively debate it didn't enjoy and can sometimes be prone to getting on its soapbox and sermonizing. But it's all part of its charm.

Sagittarius' aim is rarely to aggressively compete or make others feel unintelligent. It's an explorer by nature, and the open exchange of ideas is part of its astrological imperative. There can be a great interest in philosophy, religion, spirituality, morals, ethics, travel, and foreign cultures. Sagittarius is often known as "the wanderer" and rules the thighs in our physiology. It's simply here to search for answers to life's more significant questions.

In addition, we can't really talk about Sagittarius without talking about an inborn love for risk-taking. Ruled by lucky Jupiter, speculation is the name of the game for the archer. It moves boldly in the world, shoots its shot, and can be subject to measurable gains and significant losses. Thankfully, Sagittarius is blessed with a happy-go-lucky demeanor which means the pitfalls rarely ruffle its feathers. It just picks itself up and keeps on keeping on. "You win some, you lose some..."

MEET JUPITER

Jupiter is the planet of luck, expansion, growth, and prosperity. Jupiter also symbolizes generosity, generating almost twice as much heat and magnetism as it receives from the sun. This planet teaches us the value and symbiosis in giving. We have to be able to give to receive. Jupiter is also often linked to systems, world affairs, foreign travel, philosophy, religion, higher education, and law. In short, it's responsible for all the ways we expand. Whatever Jupiter touches gets made bigger." In modern rulership, Jupiter rules Sagittarius (expansion on the physical plane), and in traditional rulership, it rules Pisces (expansion on non-physical planes). Where we find Jupiter located in our natal charts is there we have a wealth of opportunity and luck.

Jupiter takes roughly 12 years to complete an orbit, and it expands us in 12-year cycles as well. We've spoken a bit about profection years. Jupiter Returns mark a full journey of profection years throughout the house system. This means they will always occur around the time of 12th or 1st House profection years. It's a really poetic time of endings and new beginnings. We also experience personal Jupiter squares approximately every three years and a Jupiter opposition roughly every six years, which help push us towards those more significant 12-year expansions. You can think of them as little "Jupiter check-ins." Astrology is a great clock/calendar.

So, if you think back to who you were at around ages 12, 24, 36, etc., you can look at how your life has gotten bigger. Remember, Jupiter/Sagittarius is a bit of a storyteller. The day-to-day stories we tell ourselves also work in these 12-year cycles. So look at where Jupiter falls in your chart, and think back to 12 years ago. What stories were you telling yourself then? How have those themes gotten bigger? For example, Jupiter falls in the 8th House in my chart. So, my Jupiter themes deal with things related to intensity, the occult, shared resources, and claiming personal power. When I was 12, I started dabbling in witchcraft after watching The Craft obsessively (it was the 90s...). When I turned 24, I started my first job in Corporate America, and I hated it. I felt so powerless. So, I started diving more heavily into astrology and tarot in my spare time. During my Jupiter opposition at age 30, I started The 8th House. At my Jupiter square at 33, I quit my corporate job to be in the shop full time. Now, coming up on another Jupiter Return year, I'm considering relocating the shop to a more permanent "home" to start a new phase. It's uncanny how these cycles work...

IT'S JUST A PHASE...
SAG SEASON MOONS (IRL)

> During Sagittarius Season, we typically experience a Sagittarius New Moon and a Gemini Full Moon.

SAGITTARIUS NEW MOON

Sagittarius is nothing if not optimistic and go-with-the-flow. So, during Sagittarius new moons, release the idea that you need to be too rigid or too in control. Open yourself up to a sense of adventure. Abandon the structure of your daily life (just a little). This period is about learning to sync ourselves up or plug ourselves into the natural rhythms and opportunities the universe presents to us. We often forget that we're "here for the ride." You might find that when you loosen the reigns a bit and go with your instincts, things just sort of fall into place. That's the magick of Jupiter/Sagittarius. They truly are the luckiest ducks, and when the sun and moon are both in Sagittarius, we all get a little taste of that. This is also a significant period to get in touch with the larger beliefs you hold and speak that truth out in the world. It's a time for socializing, exploring, and sharing. Enjoy it!

GEMINI FULL MOON

Following a period where we are implored to push our boundaries, take chances, accumulate and share information, and engage in a way that bolsters more extensive public awareness, the Gemini Full moon says it's time to pull inward. Remember the difference of scale in the Gemini and Sagittarius polarity. We're being pulled into more granular exploration under the Gemini Full Moon. There's a critical difference between knowledge and wisdom. Objectively knowing something is different from having a deeper internal understanding of what that thing means. The Gemini Full Moon is a time for solitude and breaking down the larger ideas we explored in the Sagittarius New Moon. We're meant to get into the "nitty-gritty," explore what these large ideas really consist of, and integrate these concepts into our lives. It's about reflection, nuance, and discernment. Jupiter/Sagittarius energy can be foolishly optimistic from time to time, and the Gemini Full Moon acts as a sort of quality control check to ensure we don't have our rose-colored-glasses glued to our faces.

WELCOME HOME
THE 9TH HOUSE (IRL) - THE HOUSE OF EXPANSION + HIGHER LEARNING

The 9th House deals with large and expansive themes such as our spiritual and religious instincts, sense of dutifulness, morals, ethics, values, and higher education. We can look to the sign on the house cusp and any planets found within the house to clue us in on the specifics of what that might look like on a person-to-person basis.

Being directly next to the 10th House/Midheaven (the highest point on the birth chart), it's situated very close to the sky's peak at the moment of birth. It represents a sort of entrance or introduction into the larger outside world. This house describes how we expand. It's about attaining wisdom and opening our view of the world. A fun fact, we can also see our relationships with our in-laws in the 9th House (if we have them, of course). For example, Venus or Jupiter in the 9th House might indicate a happy and easy relationship with in-laws. In contrast, Mars or Saturn in the 9th might show more struggle in those relationships. It also speaks to what our long-distance travel experiences might be like.

Where the 3rd House is more focused on data and processing, the 9th House is here to tale that information and pontificate on the loftier ideals in life. The 9th House rules over how we integrate the tidbits of knowledge we acquire in the 3rd House into a larger overarching ideology. It houses our more comprehensive worldview and general outlook on the larger state of affairs.

Remember that the planets are the "doers" in a chart. So, people with lots of planets in the 9th House likely focus on travel, spiritual or religious organizations, or education. We tend to see jam-packed 9th Houses in the charts of teachers, spiritual leaders, diplomats, and writers. This house also speaks to how generous a person might or might not be.

We experience 9th House profection years at ages 8, 20, 32, 44, 58, 68, 80, and 92. As always, we can look to the ruler of the sign on the 9th House cusp, its placement in the chart, and relevant transits for more specific information around what a particular profection year holds for us. So take a look at your 9th House. What does it say about your larger belief system and what expands you?

TAROT (IRL)
SAGITTARIUS - TEMPERANCE

Sagittarius is represented by Temperance in the Major Arcana. Many people are puzzled at why a tarot archetype known for patience and pause is associated with energetic, risk-taking, free-spirited Sagittarius.

Well, the word temperance comes from the process of "tempering." We do this a lot to metal, specifically ferrous alloys, to build strength. The metal is slowly heated to just below the melting point and gradually cooled in the air. This increases the material's durability by reducing hardness at a molecular level, and it's quite a slow process. You're probably thinking, "Why is she talking about all this?" But stay with me. I love science and real-world examples of the tarot archetypes at work. This imagery is critical to understanding the meaning behind Temperance. On many temperance cards, the artwork shows an angel tempering liquid between two cups. This card is all about striving for a more enlightened or improved state of being through alchemy (and Sagittarius LOVES enlightenment). We're undergoing a change in maturity in Temperance. The goal is to make us more patient and resilient.

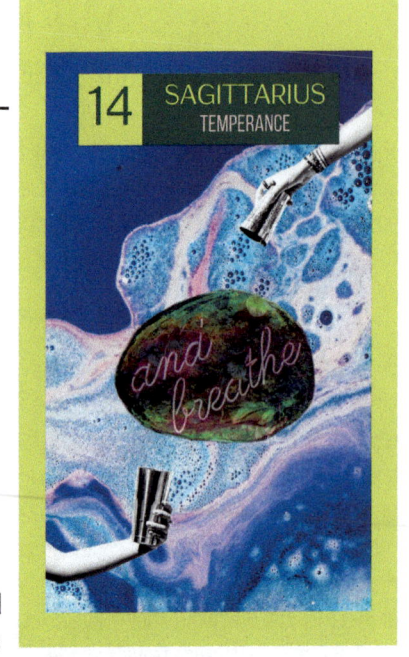

When we're in Temperance space, we're pulled to slow way down as we are tempered and shifted into the wiser, more evolved, and enlightened versions of ourselves. This card is sandwiched between Death and The Devil. We come out of a period of creating space in the Death card. We've released something in order to redirect resources and create space for something new. We're in a place where we have to mature and integrate the lessons learned before we're ready to face our shame cycles in The Devil. The imagery of tempering metal is really a good picture of what's happening in Temperance. We're undergoing an alchemical transformation to learn about the value of patience and intention.

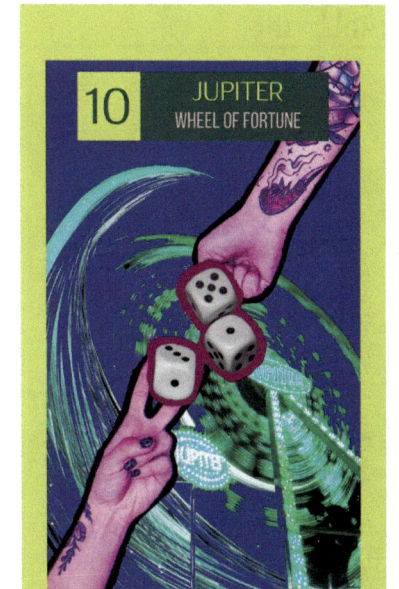

JUPITER - WHEEL OF FORTUNE

Jupiter's card in the Major Arcana is The Wheel of Fortune. If you look into traditional writing on this card's meaning, you'll see that it's tied to luck, shifts in fortune (both good and bad), falls from grace, cycles of life, and karmic balance. It feels very "What goes up, must come down." However, I'm not a huge fan of card interpretations that remove our sense of agency. There's personal agency in everything, even astrology and tarot.

So, what if we looked at this archetype from a slightly different perspective? There's a saying that "success is where preparation meets opportunity." This implies that we work hand in hand with the universe to create our reality. This is actual manifestation. Think about it. If we say we want something but do zero preparation for that thing, it doesn't matter how many "lucky" opportunities the universe puts in front of us. We won't be ready.

Conversely, if we're so tied to "the plan" and our sense of control that we're white-knuckling our way through life, our tunnel vision will make it very difficult for us even to notice the kismet the universe places in our path. Also, the universe is bigger than us. There's no way we can possibly control everything, no matter how hard we try.

The Wheel of Fortune reminds us of the space between these two mentalities. When we want something, we need to speak it into the universe and take the necessary action to work towards achieving it. However, we also must remain open and flexible to what the universe throws our way.

So, when this card pops up, ask yourself about your relationship to control. Are you doing too much or too little for what you say you want? If so, how might you correct that imbalance?

THE KNIGHT OF WANDS - MUTABLE FIRE

All of the knights in the court describe qualities of movement. We're moving boldly and impulsively, propelled by fiery passion when embodying the Knight of Wands.

Knights represent teen/adolescent energy, which is exciting but can also be inexperienced. The Mutable Fire energy implies that we're operating from a place of unrestrained fervor. This archetype represents those moments in life when the fire in our guts tells us we need to act on something immediately. When we're in the Knight of Wands space, we're highly motivated, but we likely haven't thought about the potential outcome of our actions. So while this knight can be highly effective in going after what it desires, it can also be prone to recklessness.

This card shows up during the moments in life when we need to be brave, rebellious, heroic, free-spirited, a smooth-talker, or even a bit hot-tempered. This knight is almost always associated with adventure and travel. But, if we're being honest... there's a little bit of fuck boy (independent of gender, of course) energy present within the archetype as well.

Have you ever taken a spontaneous road trip with a friend? Have you had a one-night stand on a whim because you were swept away in the passion of a moment? Have you ever marched into your boss's office and confronted them about the email they just sent without regard for the consequences? If so, then you've experienced the Knight of Wands IRL. While all of those examples hold a certain amount of risk, they also hold rewards. That's the fine line we walk under the Knight of Wands. So, when this card shows up, roll the dice!

MEET THE COURT (IRL)
MEET THE KNIGHT OF WANDS (IRL)

Use the camera on your phone to scan the QR code and access blogs where we'll discuss real life examples of the Knight of Wands.

---

8 OF WANDS - MERCURY IN SAGITTARIUS

MOVEMENT - ACTIONS SET IN MOTION

After moving through a period of defensiveness (and maybe even a little paranoia) in the 7 of Wands, we find ourselves in the 8 of Wands.

This card is all about movement. It typically depicts 8 wands flying through the air, and it implies that there's a certain irrevocability once specific actions have been set in motion. Think of a bullet fired out of a gun. Once the weapon is fired, there's no way to reverse what's about to happen. It simply has to run its course.

Remember that the story arc around the wands suit deals with chasing after something we're passionate about. So, in this case, we can think of the 8 of Wands as a moment where we become irreversibly committed to what we're going after.

9 OF WANDS - MOON IN SAGITTARIUS

PERSISTENCE - PERSEVERANCE - GRIT

After recommitting ourselves to the mission at hand in the 8 of Wands, the 9 of Wands represents a period where we need to display grit.

This archetype frequently reminds me of when distance runners "hit the wall." The body depletes its glycogen stores when we hit the wall, and intense fatigue sets in. But, for many runners, if this happens during a race they've spent a long time preparing for, there's only one thing to do. Push through the feeling, however unpleasant.

The 9 of Wands is a hopeful card. It indicates that we've faced a great deal of adversity and conquered a number of obstacles in our journey. It usually represents the halfway point in a struggle. It conveys exhaustion but also the knowledge that we will get through this.

10 OF WANDS - SATURN IN SAGITTARIUS

BURDEN - OBLIGATION - BURN OUT

After pushing through in the 9 of Wands, we find ourselves in the 10 of Wands. This card typically displays someone laboring to carry a large bundle of 10 wands, representing the heavy burden of success.

Sometimes we think we want something so intensely, but when we reach our goal, we're finally privy to the unseen struggles that come along with it. In the 10 of Wands, we've worked incredibly hard and achieved the thing. But now, we have A LOT more responsibilities.

I always think of small businesses that dream of making it big. But the more they grow, the more they realize how unsustainable the growth is as an army of one. We can't always be the problem solver or the responsible party. We need to learn to ask for help and delegate. This may mean relinquishing some of our control or power, but it's the only way for success to be sustainable.

PRACTICAL MAGICK
DEAR JUPITER ...

We know that Jupiter works in 12-year cycles. So, we're going to do a little activity. You'll need a pen, something to write on (you want to be able to rip out the pages), a candle, a jar or container, and your brain.

1. Think of one or two prominent themes in your life at the moment, and write them down. The next part is trickier because it requires us to exhibit emotional intelligence. Think of 5-10 adjectives that describe your current feelings around these themes. There are no wrong answers, but you want them to be as honest as possible. Write those down as well. We'll come back to this.

2. Now, think back twelve years. What themes were you dealing with then? I bet they're related to the current themes you identified above. Write those past themes down too. Now, I'm going to challenge you to time travel in your mind a bit. Try your hardest to put yourself in the past. What did the world look like through your eyes back then? What were your motivators? I bet they've changed since then. Think of 5-10 adjectives that describe how you were feeling 12 years ago. Write them down.

3. Now, let's come back to the present. We're going to write a couple of letters. The first is to our past selves. Tell the past version of you all the things they can't possibly know about how your life has unfolded, primarily related to the themes you wrote in steps 1 and 2. Speak to those feelings you wrote down. Even though things aren't perfect (because they never are), I bet there's some pretty amazing and expansive stuff that you could never have seen coming. Hang onto this letter. We'll come back to it.

4. One of my favorite astrologers says that the planets are here to help us, and all it requires is that we ask. She says that the planets understand ritual as an intention-filled language. So, now we're going to write a letter to Jupiter related to the themes you wrote down in steps 1 and 2. Speak to those feelings you wrote down. First, talk to Jupiter about how far you've come in your 12-year cycles and what you're presently struggling with. Thank Jupiter for all the expansion in your life to date. Now, the most important part, ask Jupiter to present you with the opportunities for the highest good for the collective, whatever they may be. We have to be open that the outcome may not be something we originally had in mind. Sometimes Jupiter knows best!

5. We just "earthed" the intention by writing it. Now, read the letter to yourself and then your letter to Jupiter out loud to "air" them. Next (in a safe space), you're going to burn both letters in a container and conserve the ashes to "fire" them. Store them in a jar or other airtight container. Last, take them to the nearest body of living water. Release them there to "water" the intention.

6. The last (and most important) step...Jupiter loves a celebration! Now, you're going to reward yourself for how far you've come in the past 12 years. Buy yourself a drink or a dessert, or whatever your favorite thing is, and allow yourself to feel proud for just a minute. I'm sure you've done a lot in the past 12 years worth congratulating, and Jupiter would def want you to celebrate that.

SORTED BOOKS
WE ARE WHAT WE CONSUME: A SELF-PORTRAIT EXERCISE

This was an activity I read about in a book called "You Are An Artist" by Sarah Urist Green. one of the prompts was to get to know someone better by checking out their book selection and then distilling the "essence" of the person into several stacks of books. You were then to stylize the stacks in a way that "felt like" the person and photograph the books, spines facing out. Honestly, I got lost looking at the photos of book stacks. You almost feel like you know the subject just by looking at what they're interested in and what they study. So, I challenge you to create a self-portrait from your library. You can also make one for a friend from their collection! Feel free to get creative with the style of the photo. Experiment with colors and textures. The image shown here is a portrait of some of my favorite books.

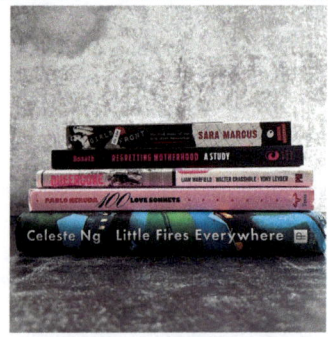

SAGITTARIUS SEASON TAROT + JOURNALING PROMPTS
ASK TEMPERANCE + THE WHEEL OF FORTUNE

These prompts are perfect for Sagittarius Season tarot or even as journaling prompts.

WHAT DOES MY RELATIONSHIP TO CONTROL LOOK LIKE? DO I TRY TO CONTROL TOO MUCH? TOO LITTLE?

HOW DO I FEEL ABOUT THE CONCEPT OF LUCK OR FATE?

HOW DO I RESPOND TO MOMENTS OF REST AND PAUSE?

WHAT ARE MY CORE ETHICS AND VALUES? HOW DO THEY DEFINE ME?

KITCHEN WITCHIN'
FAT DIP

We know that Sagittarius Season is full of gatherings and rich food. I went to graduate school in Madison, Wisconsin, and if there's a city that knows food. It's Madison. This is a dip that people in Wisconsin make all the time. Seriously, it was a party staple. Someone prepared it for basically every gathering we ever attended, and with good reason. It's delicious...and weirdly great as hangover food...

INSTRUCTIONS

1) In a large skillet, over medium-high heat, cook the sausage until crumbled and no longer pink. Drain the grease.

2) Add the Rotel into the cook ground pork and cook for 3-5 minutes on medium-low.

To finish the dip in step 4, you can use a large pan on a stovetop, but most people use a crockpot since it keeps the dip warm while it's being served.

4) Combine the ground pork and Rotel mixture with the cream cheese pieces and let the cream cheese melt. If you're using a crockpot, you can simply combine everything into the crockpot and set it to high heat for about 40 minutes to an hour. Give it a good stir, and after that, you can set it to low or warm. It's common to serve it directly out of the crockpot. If you're using a stovetop, combine the ground pork and cream cheese over medium heat until the cream cheese is melted. Stir it up, and transfer it to a serving bowl. Serve with tortilla chips. Leftovers can be stored refrigerated in an airtight container and reheated in the microwave.

As a bonus, leftover Fat Dip is often served with eggs and toast in the morning. It makes seriously great hangover breakfast food.

INGREDIENTS

- Tortilla chips (The thicker ones tend to work better. This is a heavy dip.)

- 1 lb Pork Breakfast Sausage

- 1, 10 oz can of Rotel (diced tomatoes and green chilies, undrained.)

- 1, 8 oz package of cream cheese, cut into smaller pieces.

(Seriously, this is all that's in it - 3 ingredients!)

SAGITTARIUS SEASON WORDS: THE TAKEAWAY
OUR KNOWLEDGE CANNOT EXCEED OUR EXPERIENCES

The Gemini/Sagittarius polarity teaches us about knowledge and wisdom. It's one thing to know something because we've read about it or studied it but lived experience is often what cements the concepts. Because of this, a prominent part of Sagittarius' imperative is around collecting experiences. We often see Sagittarius energy as flaky and full of wanderlust in astrology meme culture, but this is a side effect of trying to do it all. Now, as humans, of course, there's no way to see and experience everything during our time on the planet. However, you can sure count on Sagittarius to try anyway!

We've established that Jupiter/Sagittarius is expansive. It's always looking for "more," "bigger," and "better." I always picture the archetype personified as a big, jolly person at a party. They're sharing an anecdote, and everyone in the room is hanging on their every word, living vicariously through the storyteller. It's certainly warm and infectious energy. On the surface, it's breezy and congenial. I would argue that the only other sign we like to watch as much as Leo is Sagittarius However, behind that friendly and easy-going outward image, there's often a struggle with boundaries and limits and a desire to be perceived as larger than life. It almost feels like there's a bottomless pit that no amount of knowledge, attention, or lived experiences could possibly fill. It's like an insatiable hunger. This drives Sagittarius to be a bit of an edgelord. We only need to look to a handful of celebrities with strong Jupiter/Sagittarius influence in the chart to detect a theme. Tyra Banks, Nicki Minaj, Raven-Symone, Britney Spears, Taylor Swift, Miley Cyrus, Sarah Silverman, Chrissy Teigan, Scarlett Johansson, and Sia are all Sagittarius Suns. Love them or hate them, there's a certain controversial quality to every name on that list, and it highlights one of the crucial defining points of the Sagittarius archetype. It's very easy to overdo it.

Throughout Sagittarius Season or Jupiter transits, it's essential to keep in mind the balance between allowing ourselves room for growth and exploration and being careful not to take things too far. Sometimes I think about the 70s. Everyone hitch-hiked everywhere. I think that could have been a really cool experience in some ways. But, if you listen to true crime, you know what happened to many hitchhikers. Experience truly is the best teacher, but we also need to remember not to be foolish.

SAGITTARIUS

A hot air balloon -
 Floating over great expanses. (The thrill of a bird's eye view.)
An ivory pill bouncing along a roulette wheel -
 "Winner, winner! Chicken dinner!" (Some of the worst odds, with a 7.89% house edge. But fortune favors the bold...)
Spontaneous road trips -
 Sour Patch Kids and Soda. Where are we going? (It doesn't matter. Let's have an adventure.)
Logical fallacies -
 Straw man, Red Herring, Slippery Slope...("Well, actually....")
1000-piece puzzle -
 Zoomed in close on a single piece, there's no way of determining what the larger image will be. (Only in connecting all 1000 pieces do we see the big picture clearly.)
Bibliophile -
 Paper books, e-books, audiobooks. (The more you know...amiright?)
A captivated audience -
 Storytelling is truly a lost art. (It's about showing, not telling.)
Edgelord -
 Heretic or Truth-teller? (Semantics...)
Seinfeld re-runs -
 It's not about the trite or mundane problems. (It's about the principle of the thing.)
A debate team captain takes the podium -
 A lawyer approaches the bench. They say not to argue with people whose opinions you don't respect. (But, for you, I'll make an exception.)
An F. Scott Fitzgerald character -
 Jay Gatsby, the single most hopeful human in American Literature. The facade of glitz, glamour, and excess in the roaring 20s, and a not so thinly veiled message that the American Dream is ultimately unattainable. (But, without optimism, there is no story.)
A parent criticizes their child -
 "When will you settle down and get a real job?" A Chanakya quote as a retort, "One whose knowledge is confined to books and whose wealth is in the possession of others, can use neither his knowledge nor wealth when the need for them arises." (You'll never box me in.)

153

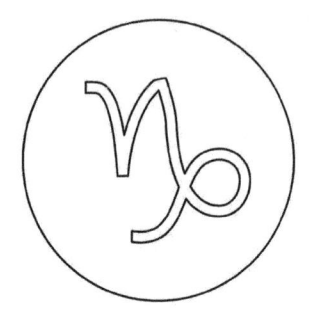

CAPRICORN

- **DATES:** DECEMBER 22 - JANUARY 19
- **ELEMENT:** EARTH
- **MODALITY:** CARDINAL
- **RULING PLANET:** SATURN
- **HOUSE:** TENTH
- **PHRASE:** I UTILIZE
- **GLYPH:** THE SEAGOAT
- **TAROT CARDS:** ACE OF PENTACLES, 2 OF PENTACLES, 3 OF PENTACLES, 4 OF PENTACLES, PAGE OF PENTACLES, KING OF PENTACLES, AND THE DEVIL

CAPRICORN SEASON PLAYLIST
USE THE CAMERA APP ON YOUR PHONE TO ACCESS THIS PLAYLIST.

CAPRICORN - A BRIEF INTRODUCTION

After the Mutable Fire of Sagittarius Season, The Winter Solstice marks the start of Capricorn Season. Capricorn is Cardinal Earth energy. We tend to think of the Capricorn archetype as a penny-pincher, and there's a good reason. However, if we remember that the shared themes of the Cancer/Capricorn polarity are stability and security, and we consider the historical implications of the time of year Capricorn Season represents, it all makes sense.

Late December kicks off the coldest part of the year in the Northern Hemisphere. So, we must be aware of the resources we have on hand. Historically speaking, prior to globalization we would have harvested and planned for the resources we needed in Virgo Season and allocated them in Libra Season. Now, it's critical that we make everything last until Spring. This is where the penchant for conservation comes into play. Capricorn has a natural sense of structure and pacing central to the archetype, and it's because our survival would have depended upon it. It's not about being "cheap." It's about forward-thinking. It's a "we might need this later, so we better hang onto it" mentality.

When we consider what this looks like in modern times. This is broke bitch season... straight up. The holidays are over. Many of us have spent more money than we probably should have. The Gregorian New Year also falls during Capricorn Season, and you know what that means - New Year's Resolutions. Often, we see people making resolutions around their personal finances during this time of year. "I'm going to budget better" or "I'm going to stash $XX.XX away in savings every paycheck." Conservation seems to be at the collective forefront during Capricorn Season, and it makes a lot of sense.

Speaking of resolutions, Capricorn is also notorious for its sense of drive and ambition. This tends to be a time of year when we set personal and career goals for the upcoming Gregorian Calendar Year. This is Capricorn's area of specialty. They're great at setting a goal and making measured progress towards it. So, it totally tracks that this is the time of year for resolutions and "getting our shit together." This is the stuff that Capricorn lives for! So, break out your draft 5-year plan. It's Capricorn Season!

CAPRICORN (IRL)

We need to have some real talk around the Capricorn archetype. Astrology meme culture paints Capricorn as being incredibly reputation-focused, capitalistic, and greedy. If the only information you had about Capricorn was from social media, you would assume that every Capricorn is like Jeff Bezos - focusing only on career, public image, and money.

Hopefully, you've realized that every sign, planet, and house has its gifts and challenges at this point in the book. So, yes, there are Capricorns out there with big Daddy Bezos energy. Bezos has a grouping of planets in Capricorn (Mercury, Sun, and Mars) in his 10th House (Capricorn's House in the flat chart) for those who aren't aware. So, he's become a sort of poster child for what the archetype represents. Although I would argue, he's only a poster child for some of the less desirable qualities.

However, we often forget that Capricorn is the sea-goat. This implies that there's an underlying watery, empathetic quality to the archetype that isn't often discussed. There's something I've noticed over the course of reading hundreds of birth charts. People with heavy Capricorn influence in their charts are great in careers that require patience, non-reactivity, and an ability to provide consistency and structure. This is what the Capricorn archetype looks like in real life. Many Capricorns I have read for work with folks with special needs, my partner included. When we consider the required skillset for that line of work, Capricorn is a natural fit. So, I guess I'm saying, "not all Capricorns..."

Regarding the connection to reputation and public image, as I mentioned above, Capricorn is naturally aligned with the 10th House. This is where the Midheaven in our charts is found. This represents the highest point in the sky at the time of our birth. It's the most "visible" part of the birth chart. So, yes, there is some preoccupation with how Capricorn desires to be perceived in the world. But, what I've seen most often is an intense desire to be regarded as competent. The archetype has a desire to be thought of as proficient, wherever it falls in our birth charts. Honestly, I think this is a very natural human urge. It's not about self-preservation and hiding any imperfections. It's about having our labor and expertise recognized and appreciated...and who doesn't want that?

MEET SATURN

Alright, y'all, the time has come. Yes, we're going to talk about Saturn (and Saturn Returns). Saturn is considered the last inner or personal planet. Past Saturn, we're in generational, outer planet territory. Saturn is also Capricorn's ruler or steward.

Saturn gets a bad reputation in astrology. It's often associated with limitations and restrictions. As with most stereotypes, there's a tiny granule of truth there. But, the more accurate description would be that it's the planet that rules our sense of maturity, responsibility, and accountability. As not fun as all of that can be, we need it. Saturn is the reason we get up and get things done. It's why we pay our bills and show up to our commitments. We also see connections to our parents in our Saturn placements in our birth chart. It also represents our attitude and approach towards our work and career. Considering the sign, house, and aspects of our natal Saturn can tell us a lot about our outlook on work, personal responsibility, and our upbringing.

Saturn has a roughly 29-year orbit. This means that approximately every 29 years, we will experience a personal Saturn Return. You've likely heard Saturn Return horror stories if you've studied astrology. I'm not here to say that they're always the easiest thing to go through, but they're here to help us.

Saturn cycles align with the natural phases of maturity in the human life cycle. We're adolescents from the time we're born until we experience our first Saturn Return at 29. Many of us live on our own and pay bills by the time we're 29, but we're not the self-possessed adult versions of ourselves until we pass through the First Saturn Return at age 29. The First Saturn Return marks the threshold between adolescence and adulthood. From ages 29 through 58, we're adults. Then, at 58, we experience a Second Saturn Return. Our Second Saturn Return marks the threshold between being an adult and an elder. Finally, if we're lucky enough to see a Third Saturn Return at age 87, it prepares us for death.

Saturn Returns aren't all doom and gloom. In fact, we tend to feel a lot better after the transits. This is because Saturn assists us in making the necessary changes to take responsibility for ourselves, and if we know anything about change, it's that it's not always comfortable. But that doesn't mean it's not necessary.

IT'S JUST A PHASE...
CAPRICORN SEASON MOONS (IRL)

> During Capricorn Season, we typically experience a Capricorn New Moon and a Cancer Full Moon.

CAPRICORN NEW MOON

Capricorn New Moons tend to fall close to the Gregorian New Year. They are a time to buckle down and set goals to work towards. This is the time to exercise a sense of structure, discipline, responsibility, and ambition. Maybe your personal budget needs attention, or you want to start a new exercise regimen, or you have a professional project you want to buckle down on. The sun and new moon in Capricorn are the perfect astrological weather for making the plan and setting the pace. The period that follows is the time to get busy and do the work. Think about who and where you want to be in the future. Think about the resources at your disposal. Remember, Capricorn's phrase is "I utilize."

CANCER FULL MOON

The Cancer Full Moon comes during Capricorn Season to provide us with a counterbalance. With all this focus and effort on our earthly and tangible stability, we must remember that it's all worthless without being in touch with our emotions and loved ones. This full moon reminds us that we don't always have to be strong. We're encouraged to let our guard down, be vulnerable, and create space for home life and social life. It's all about striking the right work/life balance. We're invited to look compare how much importance we place on our larger public reputation and tangible achievements versus what the people closest to us in our lives think of us. This full moon acts as a little pause to rest, get back in touch with the important stuff, and feel our feelings again.

WELCOME HOME
THE 10TH HOUSE (IRL) - THE HOUSE OF REPUTATION

Capricorn is associated with the 10th House. It's often called the "House of Career and Public Reputation." The main areas of focus for Capricorn Season and the 10th House are personal ambition, how we're publicly perceived, and career aspirations.

The sign that sits on the cusp of the 10th House in our natal chart is what we refer to as our midheaven. It represents the highest and most visible point in the sky at the time of our birth. This can give us information about the public image that we wish to consciously project into the world. For instance, someone with a Taurus Midheaven might prefer to have the public perceive them as wealthy, stable, and possessing a strong sense of aesthetics. On the other hand, a Gemini Midheaven might desire to be perceived as witty, curious, and intelligent. You get the idea.

If the sign on our 4th House cusp speaks to our roots and where we come from, then the sign on our 10th House cusp tells us where we're going, and it's interesting to note that the two will always be opposite by design. So, if someone has a Libra 4th House, they were likely raised in a conflict-avoidant environment, valued cooperation over competition, and focused a great deal on charm and appearances. As a result, they would have an Aries Midheaven, indicating a desire to be more publicly authentic, competitive, and assertive in their public adult lives.

We experience 10th House profection years at ages 9, 21, 33, 45, 57, 69, 81, and 93. Our focus shifts to our public image, career, and ambitious desires during these years. You can also look to transits through this house for additional information on themes that might arise during a 10th house profection year.

The planets are the "doers" in a chart. So, a chart with many planets in the 10th House indicates that the person focuses quite a bit of energy on 10th House themes - career and public persona. The planets found there tell us a lot about how that looks on an individual level. For instance, if Venus is in the 10th House, the person might leverage their relationships to help them achieve their career goals and upward mobility. There may even be a preoccupation with social standing. Look at your 10th House. What does it say about how you wish to be perceived?

TAROT (IRL)
CAPRICORN - THE DEVIL

The Devil is one of those cards that looks really gnarly and scares a lot of people. But, the meaning behind it is far less menacing than the imagery might initially convey. The traditional artwork on The Devil Card shows two naked people chained to a platform that Baphoment is perched upon. They appear to be stripped of their sense of power and personal agency. Their nudity implies that they are exposed and ashamed. But, here's the important part. Each person has a free hand that isn't bound. If they wanted to get free. They could simply unlock the chains using their free hands. The imagery implies that we are The Devil and the captive. We are responsible for imprisoning ourselves.

The Devil represents our relationship to oppression and shame cycles. You can think of The Devil as all the ways that we hold ourselves back and keep ourselves small. The big ask in The Devil is: Are we ready to unchain ourselves? That can look different from situation to situation. Maybe we're deciding to be honest and unapologetic about the thing we hold shame around. When we accept ourselves, we unchain ourselves. Or maybe we're finally willing to acknowledge and address a behavior that's holding us back. Either way, it's about reclaiming authority over our life.

It's interesting the The Devil is tied to Capricorn for two reasons. First, Capricorn can be a somewhat dominating and inflexible archetype, which certainly resonates with the concept of stripping another of their power in order to control or influence them. Second, we know that Capricorn is tied to lofty ambitions and reputation. So, The Devil almost always feels like the person who self-sabotages before they even try to go after the thing they want. Because if you don't try, then you can't fail.

SATURN - THE WORLD

The World represents Saturn. The World is the last card in the Major Arcana, and it signifies a completion, endings, and a sense of wholeness.

The traditional artwork on this card depicts the world with a person dancing in front of it, holding two wands in their hands. There's a wreath bordering the image, representing success and completion. An eagle, a lion, a bull, and a water-bearer are found in the four corners of the card representing the four fixed astrological signs - Scorpio, Leo, Taurus, and Aquarius and the four elements.

The Fool's Journey of the Major Arcana is something we're engaging in repeatedly throughout our lives. We're learning multiple lessons in perpetuity, and we're at varying degrees of progress regarding each journey or cycle we're engaged in. When we reach The World, we've finally completed a milestone for a given cycle, and it's time to jump right back into another Fool's Journey to discover something new. As long as we're alive, we're constantly learning and evolving.

When The World shows up in a reading, first thing's first, it's time to pause to celebrate. We often forget about this part. The World is a celebratory card. The work you've put in has paid off. Your efforts haven't been in vain, and you have cultivated a sense of resilience. Enjoy the moment.

It makes sense that Saturn represents The World. Significant achievements and milestones require a lot of effort, and Saturn is the planet that embodies hard work. The World illustrates the reason(s) behind why we put in work. It's the trophy at the end of the race, the prize we have our eye on, and the pot of gold at the end of the rainbow.

THE PAGE OF PENTACLES - CARDINAL EARTH

Who is the Page of Pentacles? This page is loosely aligned with Cardinal Earth Energy. They're a double earth combo. It's also youthful energy. They feel young, fresh, and inexperienced - ambitious and hardworking, yet still in the process of getting a grasp on the earthly aspects of their skills.

This is the essence of fresh earth baby energy. There's no shortage of ambition or desire for material wealth and experiences. This page is captivated by all of the tangible possibilities on the physical plane. But what this page has in studied information, they lack in real-life experience. They have the want, but they don't necessarily have a solid understanding of the how yet.

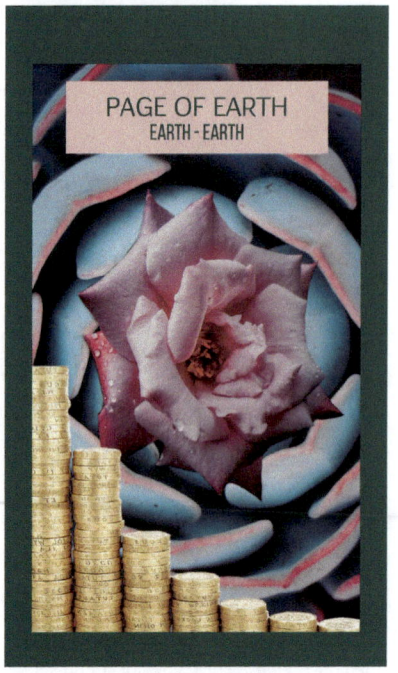

This page shows up when we're in the early stages of going after our earthly wants. Maybe we have our sights set on a house or a car, or perhaps we want to start a business. The thing is, we have no idea where to start. Research is great, but it can only take us so far. At some point, we have to get out there and take action. Practice makes perfect, and we need that real-world experience. There's also a sense of overwhelm that often comes with the Page of Pentacles. There's an intense drive and a long list of things to do to achieve the goal, but the double earth energy of this page can become stressed under pressure. This page reminds us that in those moments where it feels like too much too soon, to remember that earth energy is an expert planner. It also has a natural ability to manage the resources at its disposal. It's a reminder that Rome wasn't built in a day. Sometimes we have to divide the work into smaller, more manageable chunks and ask for help when we need it.

THE KING OF PENTACLES - CARDINAL EARTH

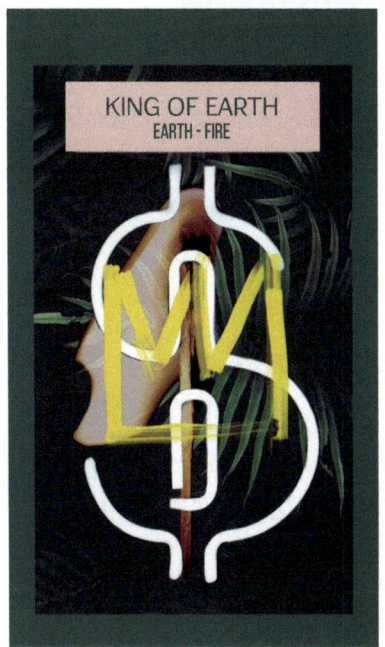

The King of Pentacles is aligned with Cardinal Earth energy, blended with fire energy. This manifests as a mature blend of ambition, planning, security, and generosity.

The King of Pentacles is an actual boss, and not in the slang sense of the word. It's got lofty dreams and the creative thinking required to bring them to life. This king is trustworthy, hardworking, and built of rock-solid character. We also see the love of material wealth through a more mature lens in this archetype. The King of Pentacles understands that resources mean nothing if we're not willing to be generous. You can't take the stuff with you when you die. So, it's always best to share what we have.

This king is incredibly secure, reliable, and displays a natural sense of leadership. It provides for and protects its own, but this isn't a dictatorship. The King of Pentacles is secure in its position and encourages everyone in its orbit toward prosperity, success, and growth. This king is the embodied concept of "community over competition."

When this king shows up, we've put in the work, and now we're in a position of power. What we do with it makes all the difference. It's easy to be greedy and power-hungry, but this king reminds us that no person is above another. It's incredibly grounded and remembers where it comes from. It knows that a helping hand makes all the difference in the world when we're in need. This isn't to say we can't enjoy material success. However, our material needs are finite, and wealth-hoarding is futile. Look around. Currently, a handful of wealthy and powerful people have the means to alleviate homelessness and hunger for the global population without even making a noticeable dent in their wealth. Yet, they choose not to. This king knows better. True wealth is in community.

MEET THE COURT (IRL)
MEET THE PAGE AND KING OF PENTACLES (IRL)

Use the camera on your phone to scan the QR code and access blogs where we'll discuss real life examples of the Page and King of Pentacles.

ARIES SEASON TAROT + JOURNALING PROMPTS
ASK THE DEVIL + THE WORLD...

These are perfect for Capricorn Season tarot inquiries or even as journaling prompts.

IN WHAT WAYS DO I HOLD MYSELF BACK AND KEEP MYSELF SMALL?

WHAT AM I ASHAMED OF? WHY?

WHAT MIGHT IT FEEL/LOOK LIKE TO LIVE COMPLETELY AUTHENTICALLY AND OPENLY, REGARDLESS OF THE OPINIONS OF OTHERS?

WHAT DOES MY RELATIONSHIP TO SUCCESS AND FAILURE LOOK LIKE? HOW DO I DEAL WITH BOTH?

DO I TAKE ENOUGH TIME AND SPACE TO APPROPRIATELY HONOR MAJOR MILESTONES?

ACE OF PENTACLES - CARDINAL EARTH

NEW OPPORTUNITIES + MANIFESTATION

This ace indicates new earthly beginnings. This could be the promise of a new house, a new career, a new financial opportunity, or even a new development in our health.

When this ace shows up we can be assured that what is to come will bring us abundance and the opportunity to expand on the physical plane. But that doesn't necessarily mean it will happen quickly. This ace isn't about instant gratification. Earth signs aren't known for speed, and this isn't a get-rich-quick scheme.

In the Mundane Magick Tarot, the imagery of a seed being planted is used as a metaphor for the Ace of Pentacles. Seeds take time to sprout, but they grow and multiply with time.

2 OF PENTACLES - JUPITER IN CAPRICORN

BALANCE - PRIORITIES - RHYTHM

After the promise of fresh earthly potential in the Ace of Pentacles, we find ourselves in the 2. We have to make room in our life for new opportunities.

The traditional artwork on the 2 of Pentacles shows a person juggling two Pentacles. There's typically an infinity symbol around the pentacles, which indicates that change is the only constant in life, and we need to remember to be flexible.

We're re-prioritizing and striving towards striking a new balance in our lives in the 2 of Pentacles. It's all about give and take and finding our new rhythm as we go after a fresh opportunity.

This two reminds us that we have what it takes. We just have to get used to juggling a bit.

165

3 OF PENTACLES - MARS IN CAPRICORN

TEAMWORK - COLLABORATION - COHESION

After finding a new balance in the 2 of Pentacles, we realize that we can't accomplish everything on our own.

The 3 of Pentacles calls us to collaboration. These are the moments when we need to work together towards shared goals. We learn about active listening, understanding, and compromise in the 3 of Pentacles.

Everyone has unique knowledge and life experiences. We can't all be an expert in everything. We need input from others, and we need to be able to share what we know. In working together, everyone advances towards their goals. We all win.

There's a cohesive quality to the 3 of Pentacles. We're all bringing our best to the table in hopes of a better future.

4 OF PENTACLES - SUN IN CAPRICORN

CONSERVATION & PRESERVATION

In the 2 of Pentacles and 3 of Pentacles, we've expanded on the new opportunity presented in ace. As it relates to Earth Energy, this kind of expansion can mean that we're drained of physical energy or our bank account is looking a little low. They say it costs money to make money, and the four reminds us to pull back and conserve.

The traditional artwork on the card shows a person clutching a pentacle over their torso. There is also a pentacle under each foot and one above their head. These represent the primary energy centers in the body. The fact that the person is covering them with pentacles indicates that they are attempting to hang onto what is being sapped from them.

These are the moments where we consciously conserve. We don't want to have all of our resources depleted. There's still a long journey ahead.

KITCHEN WITCHIN'
COFFEE, NUTELLA, CHOCOLATE CHIP OVERNIGHT OATS

Capricorn is here for fuel and efficiency. These overnight oats make a perfect caffeinated and filling breakfast on the go, and they'll keep you full all day!

INGREDIENTS
- 1/2 cup rolled oats
- 1/2 cup milk of choice
- 1 tbsp vanilla yogurt
- 1 tsp instant coffee
- 1 tbsp chocolate chips
- 1 tbsp Nutella
- Sweetener of choice
- 1 half-pint mason jar

INSTRUCTIONS
1) Combine oats and milk in the bottom of the mason jar.

2) Add the yogurt, Nutella, instant coffee, chocolate chips, and sweetener (to taste).

3) Close up the jar and invert it a few times.

4) Store in the refrigerator overnight.

Oats can be served cold or warm and can be prepared up to five days in advance.

PRACTICAL MAGICK
IT'S ALL PART OF MY 5-STEP PLAN...

If we've learned anything about Capricorn so far, the archetype is excellent at setting a goal and sticking to it. But, this isn't a skill set that comes naturally to everyone. When presented with a large or complicated task, many people become overwhelmed and experience executive dysfunction. Others bite off more than they can chew, run full speed at the task, and burn out. This exercise is designed to help break down larger goals into smaller, more manageable tasks. It's also a great way to learn how to pace yourself and stay on track without becoming exhausted.

THE 5 STEP PLAN...

Use your phone's camera to scan the QR code & access this content.

CAPRICORN SEASON WORDS: THE TAKEAWAY
MANIFESTATION CANNOT EXIST WITHOUT ACTION

Ok so, this is about to get a little personal. After opening the shop, people would regularly say to me, "You're so lucky! You get to work for yourself! I wish I could do this!" I know they meant no harm. So, I never brought this up, but it used to feel so dismissive to call the work that went into the shop "lucky." I get it. Manifestation content is all over social media. So many people think that "manifesting" something means doing a stylized ritual and then sitting back and waiting for the universe to deliver the thing to us on a silver platter. But, in reality, opening that shop took months of planning, saving, and sweat equity. It meant that I worked two full-time jobs for two years to be able to afford to keep the doors open. It meant selling our home in the middle of a pandemic to create enough savings to dip into in case of emergencies. We existed (and continue to exist) in a volatile market for small businesses. It meant not having a real vacation since 2015. It meant not a single day off for years on end.

This is what actual manifestation looks like. It's not a styled flat lay with a bowl of salt, dried flowers, crystals, and hand-lettered intentions. It's hard work, which doesn't always make for the most "aesthetic" social media content. But, it's what's real.

I don't say any of this to glorify hustle culture. We shouldn't have to "hustle" and "grind" to be able to go after our ambitions, let alone put those behaviors on a pedestal. But, I have to be honest. The things I mentioned above are all true. Those are things I had to do to keep the business afloat. So, calling it "lucky" always felt like a bit of a slap in the face.

I also don't think ritual is useless, but it's certainly not the ONLY thing in going after what we want. Ritual helps focus our intention. It's a reminder of the long-term goal, and that's wonderful. But, it's useless without aligned action. Period.

There's this idea of Capricorn as a sort of "girl boss" archetype, but it's such an inaccurate depiction. Capricorn is dedication. It's sacrifice towards a goal. It's about playing the long game and hard work. It's about patience, structure, stability, discipline, conservation, and measured progress. One of the essential lessons Capricorn teaches us is that manifestation cannot exist without action.

CAPRICORN

Standardized tests -
> Studies have shown that it's statistically unlikely for two or more consecutive answers to be the same. (The tests measure test-taking ability, not subject matter proficiency.)

An owl -
> Sitting motionless for hours on end, awaiting unsuspecting prey. (Patience is a virtue...)

An old shoebox full of savings bonds -
> My grandparents bought them when I was born. (A penny saved is a penny earned.)

Negotiation -
> "I'm gonna make him an offer he can't refuse..." (Leave the gun. Take the Cannolis.)

Performance Review -
> That episode of The Office where Angela confesses, "I believe I hold up very well to even severe scrutiny." (If you stay ready, you ain't got to get ready.)

The 5 Year Plan -
> Gantt charts, emails, paretos, and project management software. (Sure, it's annoying when they use bullshit corporate buzzwords like "synergy," but they do a 401-K match...)

A squirrel's nest -
> Full to the brim with acorns, nuts, and berries. (Better safe than sorry. Winter is long.)

A fridge full of repurposed Cool Whip and Country Crock Containers -
> Why would I PAY for tupperware? This is free. (Waste not, want not.)

A grandfather clock -
> A weight-driven pendulum keeps the time. (But not without the whimsy of a little tune on the hour.)

A skeleton -
> 2 x 4's framing the inside of our homes. (We all need a little structure to stand up straight.)

Look on the bright side, they say -
> But that's not very realistic, now, is it? (I'm not a pessimist, but like my dad always says, "hope for the best, but prepare for the worst.")

AQUARIUS

- **DATES:** JANUARY 20 - FEBRUARY 18
- **ELEMENT:** AIR
- **MODALITY:** FIXED
- **RULING PLANET:** URANUS + SATURN
- **HOUSE:** ELEVENTH
- **PHRASE:** I PROGRESS
- **GLYPH:** THE WATERBEARER
- **TAROT CARDS:** 5 OF SWORDS, 6 OF SWORDS, 7 OF SWORDS, QUEEN OF SWORDS, THE FOOL, AND THE STAR

AQUARIUS SEASON PLAYLIST

USE THE CAMERA APP ON YOUR PHONE TO ACCESS THIS PLAYLIST.

AQUARIUS - A BRIEF INTRODUCTION

After the Winter Solstice, the days are getting longer, and we're starting to look to the future. Although falling in the middle of winter, Aquarius Season brings a sense of optimism. In Capricorn Season, we're focused on survival and stability. We zoom in on getting through the winter and setting goals, but Aquarius Season is where we start considering possibilities. What do we wish to be? It's a time for invention and innovation - themes that will repeatedly surface as we discuss Aquarius.

Capricorn is known for being somewhat pessimistic. It's not negativity for the sake of being negative. It's realistic thinking. It's survival-focused. When the sun takes a trip through Capricorn, we're all influenced by the shift. We become more grounded and practical. However, when the sun moves into Aquarius, it feels like a breath of fresh air. (Aquarius is Fixed Air energy, after all.) There's a laid-back and friendly vibe to Aquarius Season, which allows us to mellow out a bit and rest as we get closer and closer to a fresh astrological new year in the spring. (Yes, I know we have Pisces Season first. I didn't forget them!)

It feels like a pause if we think about the time of year. There isn't a whole lot going on. The weather is at its coldest. So, we tend to spend a lot of time indoors. This is often time alone, but that isn't necessarily a bad thing. After major goal-setting in Capricorn Season, Aquarius Season offers us the time and space to let our minds wander. We come up with creative solutions and think about the future.

We have to remember that every sign responds to the sign that comes before it. The shift between Capricorn and Aquarius represents a move from focusing on material success and resources to abstract idealism. Instead of playing by the rules (Capricorn loves rules), Aquarius asks why the rules exist in the first place. Rather than justifying everything with a "why," Aquarius considers the possibility and counters with "why not?" If Capricorn is concerned with how the public perceives us, Aquarius says, "Who cares what they think? Let's do our own thing." It's a season about releasing ourselves from restrictions, which is interesting when we remember that The Devil card in the Major Arcana is associated with restriction and Capricorn energy.

So, let's get weird. It's Aquarius Season!

AQUARIUS (IRL)

In the Aquarius/Leo polarity, Leo represents taking center stage, being seen, and letting our creative light shine outward. Aquarius values being part of the crowd, teamwork towards the common good, and turning our creative thinking inward.

This describes an interesting "contradiction" (for lack of a better word) present within the Aquarius archetype. On the one hand, it's incredibly focused on community, humanity, and friendship. These are our humanitarians of the zodiac. On the other, it's kind of a loner. Aquarius loves alone time. The sign and its modern ruler, Uranus, are also tied to technology. Uranus is often thought of as the "higher octave" of Mercury, and we know that Mercury rules over communication. Uranus and Aquarius are also universally regarded as innovators. So, this relationship to technology, especially cell phones and social media, makes a lot of sense.

There's an image or parallel I often think of related to the Aquarius archetype that I think helps reconcile the way it values the collective but also isolation. Think about a group of Gen Z people in the same room who aren't speaking but are texting one another and sharing memes on their phones. A large part of the Gen Z population has natal Saturn in Aquarius. Saturn is Aquarius' traditional ruler. This is a group of people who are very progressive and community-focused, yet on the whole, really don't like face-to-face socializing all that much. They prefer alone time and interacting via their phones and laptops (technology).

Gen Z also isn't afraid to get weird, which is another hallmark of the Aquarius archetype. I have a personal theory that TikTok is giving Instagram such a run for its money because Aquarian Gen Z (the demographic social media platforms are clamoring to target) doesn't like the over-curated and highly stylized nature of Instagram. TikTok, on the other hand, is highly authentic. It's like getting a personal look into the strange stuff we all do when we're at home and no one is watching. It feels more intimate and connected than the overly contrived flat lays and wanderlust content that Instagram prefers. The bar for content aesthetic is VERY high on Instagram. It's not about what you say but how it looks. Conversely, the bar for aesthetics on TikTok is low. It's about what you have to say. Are you funny? Are you smart? Are you creative? Do you have interesting ideas? Apologies for the tangent, but it feels very illustrative of the Aquarius archetype.

MEET URANUS

Uranus rules Aquarius in the modern rulership model. Saturn is its traditional ruler. Uranus has an 84-year orbit. Some of us will never live long enough to experience a personal Uranus Return. Uranus spends roughly seven years in each sign. This means that everyone born within those seven years would have the same Uranus sign. The sign would be a sort of "generational stamp." But, where it would be personally expressed in each individual would be determined by the house it falls within, as that differs from person to person.

In astrology, signs are like adjectives or adverbs. They describe "how" a planet will act. The houses represent the "where," as in what area of life. I look at it like this. Whatever sign your Uranus falls within marks your generation's preferences around Uranus themes. The house your Uranus falls within is where you're personally an agent working on behalf of Uranus.

Generationally speaking, Uranus represents the things a generation disrupts and rebels against. Uranus is the planet of revolution, progress, chaos, and freedom. It likes to shake things up, but it's not about pointless destruction. It's all about pushing things forward towards a better future for the collective. For example, if you are someone with Uranus in Sagittarius (born roughly between 1981 and 1988), think about your views on religion, spirituality, philosophy, morals, ethics, and higher education. There aren't many people with this placement who value traditional sentiments on any of these Sagittarian topics. This generation prefers embracing new and less conventional spiritual concepts and doesn't tie morals or ethics to traditional religious affiliation. Another interesting generational hallmark is that Uranus in Sagittarius folks are one of the most college-educated generations. They are simultaneously the generation that sees the least value in their college education, collectively speaking.

On a personal level, Uranus in our birth charts represents the area of life where we have an unsettled and rebellious streak. It's the area of life where we make our own rules and where we're innovators. It's also the area of life where we may be prone to sudden changes or upsets. So, for instance, if you're someone who has Uranus in the 4th house, you might struggle to feel "settled" in one place. Your early childhood home may have been somewhat unpredictable, and as an adult, you may move a lot and hold non-traditional views around the concept of family.

IT'S JUST A PHASE...
AQUARIUS SEASON MOONS (IRL)

During Aquarius Season, we typically experience an Aquarius New Moon and a Leo Full Moon.

AQUARIUS NEW MOON

New moons usher in the energy of fresh beginnings, and Aquarius New Moons represent a period of optimism and change-the-world vibes. This new moon is all about authenticity, liberation, freedom, and dreams for a better future. Use this time to explore how you can give your inner weirdo space to shine. What do you need to feel comfortable being the most authentic version of yourself? What parts of yourself do you mask or hide in the world. This is the time to fully integrate and embrace all aspects of yourself. It's a time for innovative problem solving and thinking about what's best for humanity. It's also a great time to become more involved in political and community organizing efforts and volunteering. Aquarius wants to build a better future for humanity. So, when the sun and moon are both in Aquarius, we feel a jolt of motivation to make change.

LEO FULL MOON

The Leo Full Moon during Aquarius Season reminds us of Leo's counterbalance. We are social creatures, and all humans want to be seen. So, it's time to take center stage! These full moons are great for romance (Aquarius isn't exactly known for being the most amorous archetype in the zodiac), theatrics, creating art (however that looks for you), and confidently asking for what our heart desires. Leo Full Moons are designed to help us step into our power. But we all know that Leo can be prone to melodrama. So we must take care to channel this dose of fiery full moon energy into something constructive, creative, and heart-centered rather than gossiping or stirring up senseless drama out of boredom. Let's "check ourselves before we wreck ourselves." We want to work with the energy of the full moon in Leo, not against it. So, channel that Leo passion into something that brings you joy! Aquarius Season often means we're spending time alone and thinking about larger humanitarian issues. The full moon in Leo reminds us that it's also essential to make space for connection, being seen, and the things that light us up!

WELCOME HOME
THE 11TH HOUSE (IRL) - THE HOUSE OF GROUPS + ORGANIZATIONS

Aquarius is associated with the 11th House in a natural chart, and it's often referred to as the "House of Social Groups and Hopes for the Collective." This is the house that represents friendship, groups, organizations, community, and dreams for the future of humanity.

The planets are the "doers" in a chart. So, when we see a chart with many planets in the 11th House, we have someone dedicating their energy to friendships, humanitarian efforts, community work, activism, and navigating organizations. This house gives us information about our views on social groups. It also tells us about the roles we naturally gravitate to within larger social organizations. Are you someone who typically takes on a leadership role? Maybe you're more of a caretaker? Our motivators for existing in groups are also indicated in our 11th House placements.

This house is all about collaboration. It's where our unique perspectives and goals merge with those of others. What we envision as a group, we work to bring to life. We pool our natural talents, labor together, and experience wins and losses as a group. This house speaks to everything from a hobby roller skating club, to a theater company, to labor unions, all the way up to major political parties. If the group or organization exists, it lives in the 11th House.

Outside of natal planets in the 11th House, transits to our 11th House and 11th House profection years help us continually evolve and refine how we deal with our sense of all the 11th House themes mentioned here. We experience 11th House profection years at ages 10, 22, 34, 46, 58, 70, 82, and 94. As always, we can look to the ruler of the sign on the 11th House cusp, its placement in the chart, and relevant transits for more specific information around what a specific profection year holds for us.

So take a look at your 11th House. What do your placements tell you about your outlook on and role within social groups and humanitarian efforts? What does it say about your hopes and dreams for our collective future?

TAROT (IRL)
AQUARIUS - THE STAR

Aquarius is represented by The Star in the Major Arcana.

The traditional artwork for The Star shows a person kneeling by a body of water, holding a container in each hand. One foot is in the water, and another is on the bank. One container pours water onto the dry land, and the other pours water back into the pool. The surroundings are lush and green.

All of this imagery conveys a sense of rejuvenation. The Star follows The Tower in the Major Arcana. The Tower's entire job is to remove things that aren't serving our best interest but that we wouldn't ordinarily let go of on our own. It's one of the most intense cards in the Major Arcana, and it often has an understandably intense effect on our nervous system. This isn't to say that it's here to hurt or harm us. In fact, it's quite the opposite. The Tower is here to help. It just might not feel great while it's happening.

We often come out of The Tower in a state of hyper-vigilance. We've been through something big, and we're waiting for the other shoe to drop. This is when we find ourselves in The Star. These are the moments where we get to heal. We see a renewed sense of hope and personal power.

When The Star shows up in a reading, we're reminded that it's normal to take time to grieve, especially when we're standing amongst the fallout of the significant unexpected losses we experienced in The Tower. But it's also essential to give ourselves the time and space to heal and regain our strength. It's a natural human instinct to prefer a sense of control and predictability. However, once we gain some clarity over the trauma of The Tower, we're able to see a brighter future that we might not have initially imagined for ourselves in The Star.

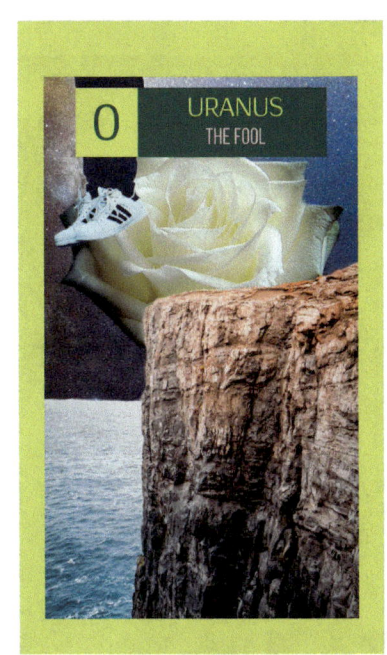

URANUS - THE FOOL

Aquarius' modern ruler, Uranus, is represented by The Fool in the Major Arcana.

Listed as Key 0, The Fool exists inside the Majors but also doesn't exist at the same time. Instead, it represents pure potential, like an unborn baby in its mother's womb.

The traditional artwork shows a person with all their belongings on their back. They hold a white rose, representing a clean slate, and it looks like the person is about to step off the cliff's edge. But to be honest, they don't seem terribly concerned. This implies a certain sense of adventure and a strong sense of naivety in The Fool archetype.

The entire Major Arcana is about The Fool's Journey. We start at this moment of pure potential in The Fool and then move through Line 1 of the Majors (The Magician through The Chariot), where we learn about ourselves. Next, we expand outside of ourselves through Line 2 (Strength through Temperance), where we learn lessons about our relationships with others. Last, we continue to expand through Line 3 (The Devil through The World), where we learn about interacting with universal forces that are bigger than us. As long as we're learning lessons in this life, we're somewhere in the Fool's Journey. We repeat the cycles through the Major Arcana over and over again as we continue to grow and mature.

When The Fool shows up in a reading, it's time to boldly "take the leap" into something new. Is it risky? Does it feel a little chaotic? For sure. But, we already know that Uranus loves to shake things up, and it's the kind of divinely-inspired chaos where we just have to jump and trust that everything will work out okay in the end.

THE QUEEN OF SWORDS - FIXED AIR

Who is the Queen of Swords? This queen is aligned with Fixed Air energy. It's an air and water combo, elementally speaking, and it feels exactly as you might expect.

The Queen of Swords isn't here for bullshit. It's a stern archetype that knows how to rely on a blend of intellect and instinct for decision-making. This queen checks in with their gut and looks at all the facts before making any moves. The archetype is a master of strategy.

Elementally, air rules over communication, and this queen doesn't mince words. Incredibly articulate, the Queen of Swords knows how to get the point across. This queen has mastered the art of direct communication and boundary-setting.

An example that comes to mind was Maxine Waters' iconic use of "reclaiming my time" during the House Financial Services Committee Hearing. When the then-Treasury Secretary, Steven Mnuchin, dodged direct questions and stalled the hearing, Waters called him out. The terminology "reclaiming my time" is rooted in traditional House Floor Procedure but has since gone viral as a symbolic way to say, "Stop screwing around. You're wasting my time and yours." This is big Queen of Swords energy.

When this queen shows up, it's time to cut the nonsense, be objective, trust our gut, say what we mean, lay down healthy boundaries, communicate directly, and take no shit. Queen of Swords energy can be especially uncomfortable for the marginalized. Yet, they are the groups who need it the most. There's a saying that "we teach people how to treat us," and this queen wants all of us to remember that we're worthy of respect.

MEET THE COURT (IRL)
MEET THE QUEEN OF SWORDS (IRL)

Use the camera on your phone to scan the QR code and access blogs where we'll discuss real life examples of the Queen of Swords.

THE MINOR ARCANA
5 OF CUPS - VENUS IN AQUARIUS

AGGRESSION - CONFLICT - INTIMIDATION

Like all 5's in the Minor Arcana, this is a contractive card. After a period of rest in the 4 of Swords, we find ourselves tangled up in some direct conflict in the five.

The traditional card artwork shows a person holding three swords. Two swords are on the ground. Two people in the background appear to have just lost a battle. The sky is cloudy and gray. The picture it paints is that this person has achieved objective victory in this particular conflict, but have they really? It feels very much like winning a battle but losing the war.

This is a time to look at the bigger picture, minimize collateral damage, and salvage what we can. We're offered a choice between collective progress or an individual win in the 5 of Swords. In life, sometimes unfair things happen. People can be cruel. Sometimes it's best to leave the score-keeping up to the universe. People tend to get what they deserve. They say, "revenge is a dish best served cold," but what if it gets us further not to serve it at all?

6 OF WANDS - MERCURY IN AQUARIUS

TRANSITION - MOVING ON - HELP + AID

After experiencing the conflict in the 5 of Swords, we learn about asking for help and the value of retreat in the 6 of Swords.

The artwork shows a forlorn person and child in a boat being rowed to land that looks more promising across a body of water. They appear to be fleeing. It always makes me think of refugees.

In the 6 of Swords, we need someone to row us to safety. The decision to make a significant transition is often not an easy one. However, retreating is also not a sign of weakness. It takes a lot of strength to make these tough choices, and it's a time when we require support.

When the 6 of Swords shows up, it's a time to move on, and it's also time to ask for help.

7 OF WANDS - MOON IN AQUARIUS

TRICKERY - DECEPTION - RESOURCEFULNESS

After retreating in the 6 of Swords, we're trying to establish our new normal. However, we're a little shaken by what we've been through so far. As a result, we have an understandably heightened sense of paranoia regarding the actions and motives of others.

The artwork for this card shows a person sneaking away from a camp. They're carrying five swords, and two appear to have fallen on the ground. The artwork conveys a sense of trying to get away with something we know is wrong.

Here's the thing, all humans are dishonest from time to time. In the 6 of Swords, it could be us or someone else. The important thing is understanding the motive behind the deception. Not all motives are created equal. The truth always has a way of being brought to light. What we do with it when it's uncovered is up to us.

PRACTICAL MAGICK
THE MAGICK OF MUTUAL AID

Things are difficult at this moment in human history. Inflation is at an all-time high. Wages are stagnant. Home prices are soaring. We're feeling the economic and emotional effects of a global pandemic. We expect that the government will come to our aid during trying times like this. This is what we elect them and pay taxes for, right? So why isn't it happening? Why are so many slipping through the cracks? If we want to see real-life Aquarius Magick in action, it's all about mutual aid. We have to lift one another up.

THE MAGICK OF MUTUAL AID

Use your phone's camera to scan the QR code & access this bonus content.

AQUARIUS SEASON TAROT + JOURNALING PROMPTS
ASK THE FOOL + THE STAR

These prompts are perfect for Aquarius Season tarot or even as journaling prompts.

WHAT MAKES ME UNIQUE? DO I SHOW THIS SIDE OF MYSELF TO OTHERS? WHY OR WHY NOT?

WHAT SOCIAL CAUSES HOLD PARTICULAR IMPORTANCE FOR ME? WHAT CAN I DO TO FURTHER THEIR MISSION?

HOW DO I ENGAGE IN MY FRIENDSHIPS AND SOCIAL GROUPS? HOW DO WE SUPPORT ONE ANOTHER?

HOW DO I MAKE ROOM FOR HEALING AND RESTORATION IN MY LIFE?

KITCHEN WITCHIN'
WE ARE THE WEIRDOS, MISTER...

Deviled eggs are already a weird (but incredibly delicious) food. So, this Aquarius season, why not take it a little further? Pickling the eggs with beets gives the egg white an intense magenta color. They look like something an alien would eat, and they're a massive hit at community events!

SPICY PICKLED DEVILED EGGS

INGREDIENTS

- 2 serrano peppers, divided
- 3 cups water
- 1 cup white vinegar
- 1 1/2 cup sugar
- 2 small beets, peeled and sliced
- 3 cloves garlic, crushed
- 3 bay leaves
- 2 tbsp whole black peppercorns
- 1 tbsp salt
- 12 hard-boiled eggs, peeled
- 2 tbsp mayonnaise
- 1 tbsp extra virgin olive oil
- 1 tbsp dijon mustard
- 1 tbsp Sriracha Sauce
- Smoked paprika for garnish

INSTRUCTIONS

1) Hard boil and peel a dozen eggs in advance.

2) Cut 1 of the peppers in half, lengthwise, and add it to a large pot. Then add the vinegar, water, beets, garlic, sugar, bay leaves, peppercorns, and salt. Bring to a boil, and then reduce the heat to low. Cook on medium-low heat for 20 minutes until the beets are tender. Remove the pot from heat and allow it to cool completely.

3) After cooling, add the hard-boiled eggs into the pot with the beet liquid and refrigerate for 6-8 hours. (I usually do this overnight.)

4) Remove the eggs, and cut them in half, length-wise. Remove and retain the yolks in a separate bowl. Place the whites on a plate or serving platter.

5) Add the mayonnaise, olive oil, mustard, and Sriracha to the yolks. Thoroughly combine everything.

6) Scoop the yolk mixture into the egg whites. Slice the remaining pepper into garnish-sized rounds, and top each egg with one. Finish by sprinkling with smoked paprika.

OUTER PLANET ASTROLOGY + WORLD EVENTS
(IT WAS ALL IN THE STARS...)

Now you didn't think we were gonna get through this whole book and not talk about the US Pluto Return and the incredibly historic outer planet astrology we're seeing right now, did you? The outermost planet movements show significant societal shifts.

SATURN-PLUTO CONJUNCTION (JANUARY 2020)
In January 2020, Saturn (the planet of structures) met up in conjunction with Pluto (the planet of power, dismantling, death, and rebirth). This marked the start of the pandemic and the collapse of many global structures and systems.

THE US PLUTO RETURN (FEBRUARY 2022)
If we were to create a birth chart for the US for July 4th, 1776, we would see that Pluto was in the late degrees of Capricorn. Guess what? As of late February 2022, transiting Pluto is back in that same position. Let's be clear. The US is older than the Declaration of Independence. There were already indigenous people, structures, and systems here. July 4th, 1776, marks the beginning of the colonial structures the present-day US is built upon, and the effects of the Pluto Return will directly affect the systems that are an offshoot of this. We've felt the impact of this Pluto Return building for several years up to 2022, and we'll continue to feel them through 2024. Pluto Returns bring down systems that aren't working. The French Revolution happened during a Pluto Return, as did the Fall of Rome (during a second Pluto Return). There are countless parallels between these historical events in human history and the current state of affairs in the US. So, if it feels like things are intense, that's because they are. Big change is happening.

OUTER PLANETS MOVING INTO NEW SIGNS (2024 - 2026)
It's incredibly rare to see all of the outer planets move into new signs back to back, but that's precisely what will happen. Pluto moves into Aquarius in 2024. This will likely bring major tech advancements, a wave of progressive policy, and a decentralization of authority. Power will likely be transferred into the hands of the people. In 2026, Neptune will move into Aries. We will probably see a big push for mental health and addiction treatment accessibility under this transit. Last, Uranus will move into Gemini in 2026. This is likely to mark changes in media (including social media) and a possible rise in cryptocurrency.

AQUARIUS SEASON WORDS: THE TAKEAWAY
POWER TO THE PEOPLE - THE AGE OF AQUARIUS
December 21, 2020, marked The Great Conjunction. Saturn and Jupiter met up in Aquarius. This astrological event only happens once every 800 years. Many astrologers are talking about how this planetary meet-up, along with the Vernal Equinox in March 2021, kicks off The Age of Aquarius. Entering a new astrological age is a big deal. We spend around 2000 years in each period. What a time to be alive, right?

We're seeing it all around us, these Aquarian shifts. On the social and political front, we're watching The Great Resignation in action. The pandemic has undeniably affected how we view our work and compensation, and people are leaving their jobs in record numbers. There's renewed focus on social justice and activism. A spotlight is shining on the glaring and impending repercussions of not acting on climate change. There's a collective call to remove power from the oligarchs and place it back in the hands of the people. The population is overwhelmingly disillusioned with the limitations of the two-party system and the electoral college's role in the US election system. Many are fighting to see the excessively wealthy pay their fair share in taxes. And speaking of taxes, there's also a growing number of the population who wishes to see major tax reform, requesting that the US simplify its incredibly complicated and expensive tax structure. There's a massive push to forgive student loan debt to provide economic relief for the generations of students who have been paying for decades, only to see the balances never budge. Union and organizing work is sweeping the country, with workers from some of the largest anti-union companies winning the union vote, seemingly against all odds.

In terms of technology (Aquarius and Uranus rule technology), we're seeing a massive shift towards utilizing technology for remote work. This is a big win for the disabled community, which has been advocating for remote work for a very long time. Also, with social distancing due to the pandemic, many of us are now leaning into our cell phones and social media spaces for human connection more than ever. We also see the rise of cryptocurrency and NFTs.

I'm not sure I mentioned it anywhere else in the section, but Aquarius and Uranus are associated with astrology, metaphysics, and parapsychology, and we see a massive increase in people exploring astrology and spirituality. So, look around. The Aquarius archetype (IRL) is happening all around us.

AQUARIUS

Cell Phones, laptops, tablets -
>All of our connections contained within a tiny square. Anything you want to know, just a quick search away. (What a time to be alive!)

UFO -
>Beam me up. (No, seriously. Do it.)

Crowds of protesters marching in the streets -
>"Show me what democracy looks like." (This is what democracy looks like.)

Modern art -
>It just looks like a replica of a toilet made out of dollar bills... (Yes, but what it is *saying*?)

Disgruntled workers marching in circles in front of a corporate headquarters -
>Signs that read "Union Busting is Disgusting" (Do not cross the picket line.)

Steinbeck novels -
>"And the little screaming fact that sounds through all history: repression works only to strengthen and knit the repressed" (...and ain't it the truth?)

Dissonance -
>A single human having 190 billion dollars while his workers struggle to afford basic healthcare. (It's cheap to be rich and expensive to be poor.)

Cryptid hunters -
>Look, in 1795, William Herschel thought the sun was cold. There was a time when we never thought we'd see a man on the moon. There's lots we don't know. (Be willing to entertain possibility.)

Social constructs -
>Gender. Money. Time. (Dismantle it all.)

Re-runs of The Golden Girls -
>The way that platonic friendships can be more intimate than marriage. (There's very little a midnight cheesecake won't fix. Thank you for being a friend.)

The do-gooder outcast -
>Caring is the new black. (Like Virginia Woolf said, "Once conform, once do what other people do because they do it, and a lethargy steals over all the finer nerves and faculties of the soul. She becomes all outer show and inward emptiness; dull, callous, and indifferent.")

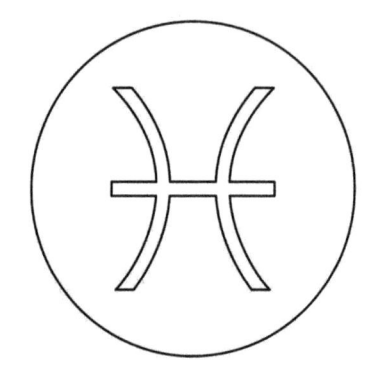

PISCES

- **DATES:** FEBRUARY 19 - MARCH 20
- **ELEMENT:** WATER
- **MODALITY:** MUTABLE
- **RULING PLANET:** NEPTUNE + JUPITER
- **HOUSE:** TWELFTH
- **PHRASE:** I BELIEVE
- **GLYPH:** THE FISH
- **TAROT CARDS:** 8 OF CUPS, 9 OF CUPS, 10 OF CUPS, KNIGHT OF CUPS, THE HANGED ONE, AND THE MOON

PISCES SEASON PLAYLIST

USE THE CAMERA APP ON YOUR PHONE TO ACCESS THIS PLAYLIST.

PISCES - A BRIEF INTRODUCTION

After being so mentally active in Aquarius Season, we enter the liminal space of Pisces Season. The Mutable Water of Pisces represents the final zodiac sign of the astrological New Year.

The word liminal comes from the Latin word for threshold. Pisces Season is the in-between space that separates one astrological year from the next. It's like sitting in a waiting room for the next astrological sun cycle. Think about elevators and airports. They hold the energy of Pisces Season. It's the tension and pliability between one space and another.

This is a time of year when we're in a holding pattern. It's too cold for springtime activities, but winter is slowly beginning to thaw away. We're at the mercy of what nature is doing all around us, and some things take time. Mutable Water represents the most permeable and fluid elemental energy. It's a season that teaches us how to go with the flow and become comfortable with waiting in the in-between spaces.

So, what do we do when we're stuck in limbo? We dream.

Pisces Season has a special connection to the dream realm, the unconscious mind, and the collective unconscious. Carl Jung's work centered on dreams. He hypothesized that our dreams were our psyche's way of attempting to communicate important information from the unconscious and that our unconscious minds were tied into a larger collective pool of unconscious knowledge containing past human experiences and universally understood archetypes. His work suggests that our dreams and day-to-day lives are full of symbolism and that nothing is a coincidence.

I'm not here to say that I think Jung was a perfect dude. He was problematic, as were many of his contemporaries. But, his work with dreams, the collective unconscious, synchronicities, and mirroring is regarded by many as the basis for why tarot and other divination methods work the way they do. We can't really talk about Pisces Season without talking about the importance of dreams, and we can't really talk about dreams without talking about Carl Jung.

So, let your imagination run wild. It's Pisces Season!

PISCES (IRL)

Pisces' glyph is two fish tied together and swimming in opposite directions. This represents that the archetype is pulled between the conscious and unconscious (dream) realms. We've talked about how each zodiac sign builds off of the sign before it. As the final sign in the zodiac wheel, Pisces has internalized the lessons of every sign that's come before it.

I often describe Pisces as being like a sponge. Because the archetype has absorbed so many experiences, it's incredibly empathetic. Somewhere inside, it can relate to everyone personally. In day-to-day life, Pisces tends to suck up people's energy, for better or worse. There's a deep sensitivity and sense of compassion present within the archetype. It's profoundly intuitive and learns through absorption. Often, Pisces has no idea where it picked up the things it knows. It just knows that it knows. This makes for a gentle and caring demeanor, but it can also give way to martyrdom. Pisces LOVES a "project." It wants to fix everyone and everything in its path, a true bleeding heart.

Pisces is also known for its unmistakable dreaminess. It can positively lose itself in fantasy, and its sense of time is, well...flexible. Pisces is the person who will text you, "I'm on my way!" and then proceed to sit in a towel and dissociate for forty-five minutes before getting dressed. Time isn't real or linear in the dream realm. So, time isn't real or linear for Pisces. It will get to it when it gets to it.

There's also a darker side to Pisces, which is seldom discussed. Pop culture astrology paints the archetype as an otherworldly, glittery, pastel, softie. But with great empathy comes great responsibility. Pisces has a heavy emotional load to bear, and it's prone to escapism. That looks different from person to person. But, some celebrities that come to mind who have heavily Piscean charts include Kurt Cobain (Sun, Mercury, Chiron, Venus, and Saturn in Pisces), Drew Barrymore (Sun, Venus, and Jupiter in Pisces), and Kesha (Sun, Moon, Mercury, and Jupiter in Pisces). Noticing a theme? They've all publicly struggled with addiction and mental health. Of course, this isn't the case for every Pisces. But it's worth noting that Pisces isn't all cotton candy and unicorns. The archetype carries a heavy weight, and without proper channels to be able to "release the collective load" in a healthy way from time to time, we see these sorts of struggles.

MEET NEPTUNE

Neptune rules Pisces in the modern rulership model. Jupiter is its traditional ruler. Neptune has a massive 165-year orbit. So, humans don't live long enough to see a personal Neptune Return. Neptune spends roughly 14 years in each sign. This means that everyone born within those 14 years would have the same Neptune sign. The sign would be a sort of "generational stamp." But, where it would be personally expressed in each individual would be determined by the house it falls within, as that differs from person to person.

In astrology, signs are like adjectives or adverbs. They describe "how" a planet will act. The houses represent the "where," as in what area of life. I look at it like this. Whatever sign your Neptune falls within marks your generation's preferences around Neptunian themes. The house your Neptune falls within is where you're personally an agent working on behalf of Neptune.

Generationally speaking, Neptune represents the things a generation collectively dreams about. It also shows where a generation is delusional and confused. In short, Neptune is the planet of hopes, imagination, and idealism. For example, suppose you are someone with **Neptune in Capricorn** (born roughly between 1984 and 2000). In that case, you're part of a generation that dreams of essential stability and security - a house, a livable salary, and affordable healthcare. Adults told Neptune in Capricorn kids to go to college. Then, they would be able to have all these things. So, they did. A substantial portion is drowning in student loan debt, being paid wages that aren't consistent with inflation, unable to afford homeownership and basic healthcare (even with insurance). These basic securities were what they dreamed of and were also where they were lied to.

On a personal level, Neptune in our birth charts represents the area of life where we are idealistic. It shows where we're creative and imaginative and also where we're prone to confusion and being taken advantage of. For example, if you have Neptune in the 7th House, you are likely in love with love. However, you might approach relationships with rose-colored glasses on, and you and your partner might not see each other clearly. Or let's say you have Neptune in your 3rd House. This would indicate a person who spends a lot of their time daydreaming and might struggle with concentration. These people often have trouble communicating verbally and get their point across best via the arts.

IT'S JUST A PHASE...
PISCES SEASON MOONS (IRL)

> During Pisces Season, we typically experience a Pisces New Moon and a Virgo Full Moon.

PISCES NEW MOON

The Virgo/Pisces polarity shares the theme of devotion. Virgo deals with being of service on the physical plane, and Pisces focuses on faith and dedication on the intangible plane. It's about believing in the things we can't perceive with our five senses. So, the Pisces New Moon is a period of significantly heightened intuition. Pay close attention to your dreams during this time. The things you're dreaming about around the Pisces New Moon matter. This is a great time to start a dream journal and indulge in a bit of rest. Don't pack your schedule too tightly. Not every moon phase is meant to be outwardly action-packed. Leave room to let your mind and heart wander a bit. This new moon is exceptionally sentimental. Trust that whatever comes up may help you define your feelings and get in touch with your dreams. Remember, we don't always need to see or touch something to believe it. Simply feeling it is enough, especially when the sun and moon are both in Pisces.

VIRGO FULL MOON

The Virgo Full Moon shows up in Pisces Season to help us get grounded again. Remember, we're heading into active Aries Season before we know it! So, this earthy full moon reminds us that our time in the Pisces liminal space is almost up, and it's time to start making some real-world preparations for the astrological new year. Of course, the sun is still in Pisces, so it's not all business, but it's a period for balancing systematic thinking and dreamy surrender. Pisces Season is great for listening to our intuition, and we need these moments of pause from time to time. But, the season can also leave us feeling foggy and out of touch with reality. So, this is a great time to shake ourselves out of that and start thinking about the routines we'd like to get into. We've spent all of Pisces Season leaning into our intuition and getting in touch with our dreams, and the Virgo Full Moon is the time to ask ourselves what practical steps we need to be taking to make those dreams a reality.

WELCOME HOME
THE 12TH HOUSE (IRL) - THE HOUSE OF THE COLLECTIVE UNCONSCIOUS

The 12th House is a tricky one to understand by design. It represents our direct connection to the collective unconscious. I think of it as a karmic junk drawer where we compartmentalize things. It's a liminal house where invisible enemies, trauma, suffering, psychological fears, and reckoning live. It's where we're a "behind the scenes player." We can look to the sign on the house cusp and any planets found within the house to clue us in on the specifics of what that might look like on a person-to-person basis. But, it's important to note that planets within the 12th House don't behave the way we might typically expect.

Since the 12th House has a very Piscean/Neptunian feel, and we know that Pisces and Neptune tend to warp and distort what they touch, any placements in the 12th House are sort of "turned in on themselves." An example I often use when explaining 12th House placements in readings is to imagine holding a letter in your hand. You would be able to see it, read it, and know what it says. Then, imagine submerging that same letter under a few inches of water in a bathtub. You would still know it was a letter, and you might even be able to read parts of it from time to time, but the water would distort it. That's what having planets in the 12th House feels like. (I have a 12th House moon.) We know the planets are there, and we can feel them occasionally, but the traditional descriptions of what the planet and sign combinations represent don't always resonate because the placements are distorted in some way by the 12th House.

I have a theory about charts with strong 12th House placements. The things living in our 12th Houses represent the stuff that we objectively know about ourselves and our experiences on some level. But, they're things that affect us so intensely that if we fully felt them in our day-to-day lives, we might not be able to function. This is why I refer to the 12th House as a sort of karmic junk drawer. We "throw things in there" to compartmentalize them so that we can function.

We experience 12th House profection years at ages 11, 23, 35, 47, 59, 71, 83, and 95. As always, we can look to the ruler of the sign on the 12th House cusp, its placement in the chart, and relevant transits for more specific information around what a particular profection year holds for us. So, what's in your 12th House?

TAROT (IRL)
PISCES - THE MOON

Pisces is represented by The Moon in the Major Arcana.

The traditional artwork shows a path dimly illuminated by the moon. A wolf and dog stand on either side of the trail. They are said to represent the primal and civilized parts of human nature, respectively. The path represents the divide between the conscious and the unconscious. When we're in The Moon, we're straddling this line. We're in the space between the two realms and receiving information from both sources.

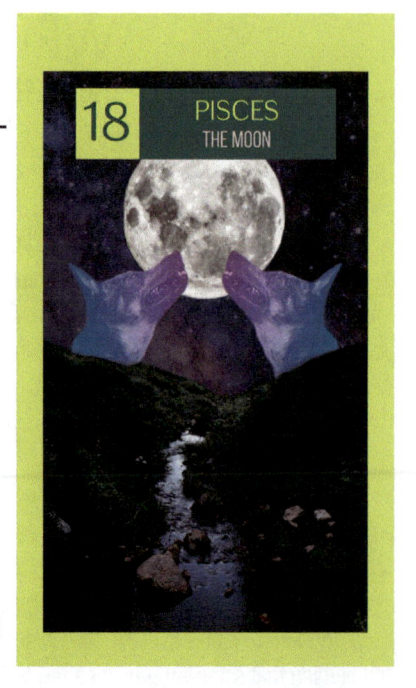

This card follows The Star. Remember that in The Star, we're recuperating from The Tower. In the Moon, we're eased back out onto our path, but it's dark. We can't make out all the things around us. So, we're relying on our instincts. We tend to feel unsure, anxious, and even a bit fearful in The Moon. There could be unseen danger all around us...or not. We're just not sure.

The moon is truly the "it's complicated" card. Under The Moon, we feel confused and uncertain. Secrets also thrive here. So, there's often a sense that we "don't have the whole story" of whatever we're working through. Sometimes this card indicates that our imagination is getting the best of us. Other times, it can indicate legitimate concerns that aren't entirely known to us yet. We also see periods where our psyche and mental health is getting the best of us.

But, not to fear, The Sun follows The Moon in the majors, and it's like they say, "What's done in the dark will always come to light." So, these periods don't last forever. Eventually, we get the clarity we're seeking, for better or worse.

NEPTUNE - THE HANGED ONE

The Hanged One in the Major Arcana represents Pisces' modern ruler, Neptune.

The traditional artwork shows a person hung upside down from their foot. They aren't in pain. Their facial expression is calm. They're hanging there of their own free will.

The Hanged One represents liminal spaces. These are the moments in life where we're not meant to have all the answers. We just have to wait, and waiting sucks sometimes. Straight up. It can be uncomfortable.

The Hanged One teaches us that there's enlightenment to be found in these uncomfortable holding patterns. We have a new perspective on the world when we're hanging upside down. We see things from a different angle and entertain new possibilities that we might not have been aware of if we hadn't been subject to this waiting period.

This card also teaches us about the power of mind over matter and not to fight the process. Sometimes in life, we have to learn to relax into the discomfort.

I used to do aerial arts in my 20s, and I was terrible about stretching. It was always so boring to just sit in uncomfortable positions and wait for slow progress. But, The Hanged One is a lot like that. The only way to build static flexibility is to get slightly uncomfortable and stay there. When you first get into a stretch, you think to yourself, "OMG, this sucks. I can't do this." But, as soon as you stop fighting it, relax, and breathe, you sink deeper into it. Over time, you build flexibility.

The Hanged One precedes The Death Card. So, enjoy this period of non-guilty reverie while you can.

THE KNIGHT OF CUPS - MUTABLE WATER

All of the knights in the court describe qualities of movement. We're moving intuitively, propelled by watery empathy when embodying the Knight of Cups.

Knights represent teen/adolescent energy, which is eternally optimistic but can also be illogical. Mutable Water energy implies that we're operating from a place of unrestrained heart and imagination. This archetype represents those moments in life when we're called to let our emotions guide the way. The course of action or the path we take may not make the most sense, but it is what we need to be fulfilled.

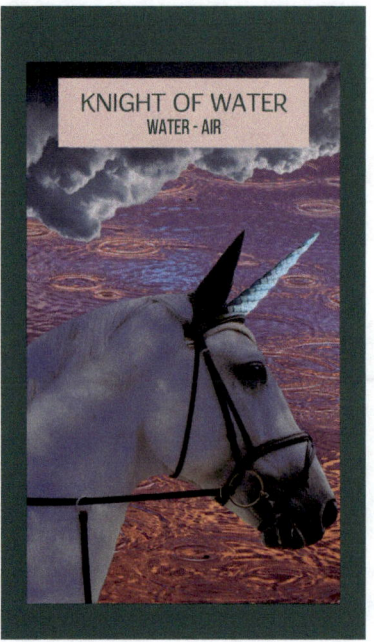

The Knight of Cups brings tremendous creative and romantic value. If the Page of Cups represents the inspiration of a new and imaginative venture, then the Knight of Cups represents being motivated to act on it.

When this card shows up in tarot readings, it's often because we're so tied up in what we think about something that we've forgotten to ask ourselves how we feel about it, which can be just as important. The Knight of Cups reminds us that we're meant to follow our hearts and emotional instincts from time to time, even if it isn't logical. Sometimes, that's where the magick is.

This knight isn't a fast-mover like some of the others. Remember, Pisces and Neptune don't have a very linear understanding of time. This isn't a journey that will be a race to the finish line. Under The Knight of Cups, we often meander. The path may be winding and a little all over the place. However, while it may not be the most efficient road to where we're going, the stops along the way are exploratory, intuitively taken, and serve the ultimate end goal. So, get comfortable with "being along for the ride."

MEET THE COURT (IRL)
MEET THE KNIGHT OF CUPS (IRL)

Use the camera on your phone to scan the QR code and access blogs where we'll discuss real life examples of the Knight of Cups.

---

8 OF CUPS - SATURN IN PISCES

WALKING AWAY & LETTING GO

In the 7 of Cups, we had several choices at our disposal. Now, in the 8 of Cups, we've made our choice, and it's time to pursue it.

This card represents a moment of transition. Sometimes we have to leave things, people, and places behind to search for truth and what's right for us.

Think of all the breakup cliches - "It's not you, it's me." or "I just need to work on myself." That's very much the energy of the 8 of Cups. We don't know what lies ahead, but we know we're not entirely fulfilled where we are. So, we have to make the decision to get out there and do the work to understand what will be a fulfilling path for us. It's rarely an easy thing to do, but it's work that's worth doing, and Saturn is the planet of work, after all.

9 OF CUPS - JUPITER IN PISCES

FULFILLMENT - SATISFACTION - PLEASURE

In the 8 of Cups, we left our familiar surroundings behind in search of higher truth and fulfillment, and in the 9 of Cups, we've found it!

The 9 of Cups shows the moments where we've found self-satisfaction. Maybe we took a risk and left a career we hated to do something we loved instead. Or perhaps we relocated to a part of the world where we've always dreamed of living, and it's everything we thought it would be.

This card is often referred to as the "wish" card. When it shows up in a reading, it indicates that the things you're dreaming about are likely to come to fruition, and they will be everything you imagine. However, there is one word of caution. We have to beware of smugness. Remember that fruit is the ripest just before the rot. So, remember to stay humble and grateful for the experience, however long it may last.

10 OF CUPS - MARS IN PISCES

LEGACY - GENERATIONAL HARMONY - ALIGNMENT

The 9 of Cups represents personal fulfillment. That energy expands outward generationally or into our legacy in the 10 of Cups.

The 10 of Cups represents the moments in life when we've experienced so much joy and fulfillment that our cup literally runneth over, and we share it with our friends, family, and the people around us. It's like a giant ripple effect. The positivity we're spreading is contagious, and everyone in our sphere supports and loves one another.

There's a sense of wholeness and completion in the 10 of Cups. Think back to the 8 of Cups and how difficult we thought it might be to leave what was familiar to us behind in search of something truly fulfilling. Now, in the 10, we see that it was all worth it in the end.

PRACTICAL MAGICK
DECODING DREAMS

Dreams are weird. It often feels like nothing makes sense. But, according to Jungian Theory, our dreams communicate essential information to us all the time. It's just a matter of being able to decode it.

This Pisces Season, try keeping a dream journal. The key is to write in it ASAP after waking up. I know it's tempting to grab your phone but don't. Once we "wake up" our conscious mind by going about our morning routine, the dream details in our unconscious mind quickly slip away. So, it's crucial to write them down while everything is fresh. If you're struggling to remember your dream, it can be helpful to remember what you were thinking about as you drifted off to sleep. Sometimes that can trigger memories.

Below are common symbols that we see in dreams with some suggested symbolism. Of course, you are the best person to attempt to decipher your dreams, but hopefully, these can lend a bit of a helping hand.

- Animals in our dreams often symbolize the primal or animalistic part of ourselves or others. Some dream interpreters believe that being chased by a predator in our dreams indicates that we're holding back or repressing emotions such as fear, jealousy, or aggression.
- Pregnancy and babies often signify fresh starts or new beginnings.
- Being chased often shows that we feel threatened in some way.
- The death of friends or loved ones often indicates change. It's not necessarily a psychic prediction. It typically just shows that a relationship is changing.
- Falling in our dreams often indicates feelings of failure, loss of control, or anxiety. It shows that we might be uncomfortable with the idea of letting go.
- Houses are said to represent our inner psyche. So pay attention to the symbols and decor. It can say a lot about emotions and memories.
- Killing someone or something in our dreams doesn't mean we actually wish to commit murder. Instead, it can represent periods where we want to "kill" a part of our personality or a cycle in our lives.
- Sex dreams can indicate a desire for intimacy, physical or emotional.
- Teeth and the loss of teeth are very common in dreams, and it is said to represent insecurity.

A PISCES SEASON FILM FESTIVAL
ENTERTAIN YOURSELF IN THE LIMINAL SPACE

While we're enjoying a little time in the in-between space, why not entertain ourselves? Pisces Season is a great time to treat yourself to some existential cinematic treats. Below are some of my favorite films that carry BIG Pisces/Neptune energy. Enjoy!

1) The Science of Sleep - It's a surrealist comedy about a graphic designer who's dreams and overactive imagination begin to overtake his waking life. (It's very cute.)
2) The Fountain - It's described as "an epic magical realism romantic drama." Without giving too much away, it depicts the nonlinearity of love, life, death, space, and time in some of the most dreamy and beautiful cinematography.
3) The Virgin Suicides - This is probably the best film Sofia Coppola has ever directed. It follows the lives and deaths of 5 sisters in the mid-70s, as told through the overly-idealistic eyes of the neighborhood boys who pined for them. The entire soundtrack was done by Air (known for their signature synthy dream pop sound), and the cinematography uses a hazy cross-process filter. The entire movie feels like a dream. (TW: This movie deals with themes of suicide, so use discretion.)
4) Eternal Sunshine of the Spotless Mind - After a breakup, a couple undergoes a fictitious medical procedure to erase one another from memory. This one will get you in your feels. It gets me every time.

PISCES SEASON TAROT + JOURNALING PROMPTS
ASK THE MOON + THE HANGED ONE

These prompts are perfect for Pisces Season tarot or even as journaling prompts.

HOW DO I REACT TO UNCERTAINTY?

WHAT ARE MY FEARS AND ANXIETIES? HOW MIGHT I BEST COPE WITH THEM?

HOW CONNECTED AM I TO MY DREAMS? ARE THERE RECURRENCES? WHAT MIGHT THEY MEAN?

WHERE COULD I USE A NEW PERSPECTIVE?

KITCHEN WITCHIN'
LAVENDER MACARONS

We know that Pisces and Neptune rule over the dream realm. So, you know I had to select a recipe with a lavender twist. These sweet, adorable, and delicious macarons positively embody Pisces Season! (And they're easier to make than you might think!) Recipe makes 30 Macarons.

INSTRUCTIONS

1) Make the macaron shells first. Combine the powdered sugar, almond flour, and 1/2 tsp of salt in a food processor. Process on low to ensure everything is well-mixed and extra fine. Then, sift the mixture through a fine-mesh sieve into a large mixing bowl.

2) In the bowl of a standing mixer or a separate mixing bowl, if you're using a hand mixer, beat the egg whites and remaining 1/2 tsp of salt until soft peaks form. Next, add the granulated sugar and beat until stiff peaks form.

3) Add the vanilla and lavender extract and food color gel. Beat until just combined.

4) Gradually add the sifted almond flour mixture to the beaten egg whites and gently fold everything in with a spatula. Transfer to a piping bag.

5) Place parchment paper on a baking sheet and pipe the macarons onto the paper in 1.5-inch circles, spacing them at least an inch apart. Tap the baking sheet on a flat surface to release any air bubbles, and then allow the macarons to sit at room temperature for 30 minutes to 1 hour until dry to the touch.

6) Bake the Macarons for 17 minutes at 300 degrees F, and allow them to cool completely.

7) Make the filling. In a large bowl, add the butter and beat with a mixer for 1 minute. Sift in the powdered sugar and beat until incorporated. Add the vanilla and lavender extract and beat until incorporated. Then, add heavy cream one tablespoon at a time and beat until the desired filling consistency is achieved. Transfer to a piping bag.

8) Assemble the macarons. Add a dollop of cream to the inside of one macaron shell, and then top it with another macaron shell to create a sandwich. Repeat with all of the shells and remaining buttercream. Allow them to rest in an airtight container for 24 hours to bloom.

INGREDIENTS

Macaron Shells:
- 1 3/4 cups powdered sugar
- 1 cup almond flour, finely ground
- 3 egg whites, room temp
- 1/4 cup granulated sugar
- 1 tsp salt, divided
- 1/2 tsp vanilla extract
- 2 drops purple gel food coloring
- 4 drops lavender extract (do not use essential oils)

Buttercream:
- 1 cup unsalted butter (2 sticks) at room temp
- 3 cups powdered sugar
- 1 tsp vanilla extract
- 3 tbsp heavy cream
- 2 drops lavender extract (do not use essential oils)

PISCES SEASON WORDS: THE TAKEAWAY
A DREAM YOU DREAM ALONE IS ONLY A DREAM. A DREAM YOU DREAM TOGETHER IS A REALITY.

Pisces Mercury, Yoko Ono, is quoted as having said this, and it reminds me of something that one of my favorite astrologers often teaches about. When the sun transits through Pisces, we collectively dream. Those dreams lay a foundation for what we want our reality to look like. So, it's crucial that we give them space.

Modern Western Culture has us convinced that unless our time is structured to maximize productivity, we're wasting it. There's a misconception that we're lazy if not constantly working. But, Neptune's job is to remind us that dreaming and non-guilty reverie are crucial in the human experience. If we're so wrapped up in doing all the time, we have little opportunity to focus on the things our unconscious and the collective unconscious are communicating to us. In short, humans simply aren't meant to be busy all the time.

I'm sure we've all wandered into a room and immediately forgotten why we entered the room in the first place. We've also had the experience of attempting to will our minds to focus on something only to find that all we're capable of is being carried off into daydreaming by even the most minor distractions. This is Neptune's way of "stealing back" the time and attention we withhold when we compulsively and excessively pack our schedules to keep ourselves productive.

Productivity is great, but if we don't take the time to check in with our dreams on what we should be productive doing in the first place, it presents a problem. Instead, we give our time and energy to the objectives of others and perpetuate the systems and structures that hold us back from going after our dreams.

So, allow yourself space this Pisces Season. Who cares if the dishes and laundry aren't done? No one will die if it waits an extra day or so. Don't make "deals" with yourself. "If I clean the bathroom, I'll allow myself an hour of TV time." Stop qualifying doing nothing with doing something. Has it ever struck you as odd that we work around the clock? Every living thing experiences busy periods and rest periods in nature. So, why do humans cheat themselves out of natural periods of rest? There are plenty of other seasons in the year designed for high productivity. Pisces Season just isn't one of them....and that's wonderful. Lean into it.

PISCES

The weightlessness of floating in water -
    Woudn't it be great to not have a body? (These flesh prisons sure are inconvenient and expensive.)
Red Room -
    The way everything and nothing makes sense in Lynch's work. (That gum you like is going to come back in style.)
Dreamy synthpop -
    Oscillators manipulating electrical voltages to produce distorted sound. (If soundwaves can be exploited, what about time and space?)
Surrealism -
    Psychic automatism removing the filter of the few social graces humans possess. (The result: some of the most fantastical and unnerving works in history. The collective unconscious must be a trip...)
Gene Wilder singing "Pure Imagination" in Willy Wonka and the Chocolate Factory -
    The way sugary sweetness can mask primitive darkness. (I've always wondered what the buttercream mushrooms tasted like.)
Unidentified alien-like deep sea creatures -
    Scientists estimate anywhere between several hundred thousand to more than 10 million unidentified species call the deepest, darkest corners of the ocean home. (Maybe there's a bit of magic in the wonder of not knowing everything. Image having nothing new to discover...)
Dissociation -
    A mind unplugged from a body and it's surroundings. (Turn on, tune in, drop out.)
The quantum phenomenon of superfluidity -
    Frictionless, zero viscosity liquid helium, as temperatures approach zero degrees kelvin. No longer individual atoms bouncing around, they behave as one collective unit, defying gravity and refusing containment by any vessel, their fundamental quantum nature altered by temperatures colder than space. (Think about the implications...we're made of atoms too, you know...)
"Be realistic," they say -
    But what is reality if not observer dependent? All experiences are merely information whirling inside our heads. Physicists have proven that the presence of extended networks of observers defines the structure of physical reality and spacetime itself. In our dreams, we simply choose to retreat from the consensus universe. (But that doesn't make them any less real.)

LINKS TO SUPPLEMENTAL MATERIALS

All of the supplemental QR-Code-linked activities can be found via the links below...

ARIES
www.shopthe8thhouse.com/aries-irl-bonus-content

TAURUS
www.shopthe8thhouse.com/taurus-irl-bonus-content

CANCER
www.shopthe8thhouse.com/cancer-irl-bonus-content

GEMINI
www.shopthe8thhouse.com/gemini-irl-bonus-content

LEO
www.shopthe8thhouse.com/leo-irl-bonus-content

VIRGO
www.shopthe8thhouse.com/virgo-irl-bonus-content

LIBRA
www.shopthe8thhouse.com/libra-irl-bonus-content

SCORPIO
www.shopthe8thhouse.com/scorpio-irl-bonus-content

SAGITTARIUS
www.shopthe8thhouse.com/sagittarius-irl-bonus-content

CAPRICORN
www.shopthe8thhouse.com/capricorn-irl-bonus-content

AQUARIUS
www.shopthe8thhouse.com/aquarius-irl-bonus-content

PISCES
www.shopthe8thhouse.com/pisces-irl-bonus-content

ACKNOWLEDGMENTS

This book is for my grandparents, who always told me that I "could do anything I put my mind to," and my family, who may not entirely understand my beliefs or my decision to leave corporate America to do The 8th House full time, but still love and support me anyway.

Honestly, many people are to thank for their role in bringing this project to life. But, I suppose I have to start with my partner, Jeremy, who has trusted and believed in me more than anyone else I know. He has uprooted his life multiple times to follow my career all over the country (and the world, for a few years there). He supported my decision to spend our life savings opening up The 8th House, and he never makes me feel guilty or neglectful for my...unconventional work hours. I don't know that The 8th House or any project I've worked on would exist without him.

As many of you know, this book was funded on Kickstarter. The writing started long before the pandemic, and the plan was to finish the book shortly after the Kickstarter closure to get it to print. But 2020 and 2021 had other plans. We sold our home. We moved multiple times. We lost a printer. Pulp prices went up. We were affected by significant supply chain and shipping delays. You name it, it went wrong. Look, I'm not a "chill girl." I like having control over my projects. So, this was a long, hard lesson about what I can and can't control. Thankfully, most of the Kickstarter backers were so incredibly understanding, and I cannot thank each of them enough for that grace. Unfortunately, this is the nature of bringing projects to life. Sometimes, everything is smooth, and sometimes everything about our plan falls spectacularly to pieces. But this is the stuff that builds resilience. So, thank you to those who believed in me enough to support the project and were so patient with all of the delays. I've wanted to write a book for a very long time, and it wouldn't have happened without all of you.

I also have to thank the folks supporting The 8th House Patreon and our kickass Discord crew. You all are like a little family to me.

And last, but certainly not least, I need to shout out a few special friends who were my sounding boards for frustrations and wins around this project. Kylee, Rachel, Jess, I would have fallen to pieces without you. Thank you so much for listening, commiserating, and reminding me that I can do this, even when I wasn't so sure myself.

ABOUT THE AUTHOR

SARA CALVARESE

Sara is an Aries Sun, Leo Moon, and Virgo Rising. She's an astrologer, tarot reader, author, tarot and oracle deck illustrator, and owner of The 8th House, a brick and mortar and full service online modern metaphysical shop rooted in prioritizing ethical sourcing, non-appropriative products, and fair compensation. A science witch at heart, she believes that science and magical practices can not only co-exist but have shared goals and complement one another. She left her 12-year career as a chemist and chemical engineer to run The 8th House full time in 2020.

CONNECT WITH SARA:

Website: www.shopthe8thhouse.com
Patreon: www.patreon.com/shopthe8thhouse
Instagram, TikTok, Facebook, Pinterest, & Vero: @shopthe8thhouse

OTHER PROJECTS:

The 8th House Tarot, An Astrological Tarot Deck
Prism Tarot
Mundane Magick Tarot
Stories: A Collaborative Oracle Deck